TEMPUS
Oral History
SERIES

BOLSOVER
voices

Bolsover Colliery in the 1970s. Castle Estate is in the foreground and Duckmanton is on the horizon. In the centre can be seen, gable end on, the original manager's house, Portland House, adjoining the colliery offices.

Cover illustration
Town End Methodist Church, 1958.

TEMPUS
Oral History
SERIES

BOLSOVER
voices

Compiled by
Bernard Haigh

TEMPUS

First published 1998
Copyright © Bernard Haigh, 1998

Tempus Publishing Limited
The Mill, Brimscombe Port,
Stroud, Gloucestershire, GL5 2QG

ISBN 0 7524 1077 6

Typesetting and origination by
Tempus Publishing Limited
Printed in Great Britain by
Midway Clark Printing, Wiltshire

Bruce Woodcock, British Heavyweight Champion and later Bolsover licensee, shakes hands with Sid Fisher in 1953.

CONTENTS

Bolsover St John Ambulance Brigade in 1968-69 with their winning trophies: the Senior Miners' Trophy, Junior Miners' Trophy, Grand Prior and the Dewar Shield. They are, from left to right: Malcolm Spencer, David Baker, Norman Bust, Michael Bust, Philip Baker, Neville Blakeley, John Spray, Ian Blakeley, Roy Madin, and Brian Wooldridge.

ACKNOWLEDGEMENTS

I would like to thank all those people without whose help this book would not have been possible. In the interval between interviews and publication some of the interviewees sadly have died. I hope this book may, in part, prove a suitable memorial to them.

Pam Ashley, 'A.W.', Ada Bagshaw, the late Bob Banner, Don Bateman, Alf Bentley, Ian Blakeley, Dorothy Cutts, Jack Elliott, the late R. Fletcher, the late Ethel Hodkin, Bessie Holmes, Betty Hunter, Marian Jones, Pete Jones, Anne Joyce, David Joyce, Joyce Leaning, Ken Leaning, Norah Ley, Roy Madin, Bunty Margerrison, the late Joe Mason, Jean Page, the late Kath Palmer, Ada Riley, Eileen Spray, the late William Spray, John Tinsley, Margaret Utridge, Anne Woodhouse.
For typing the original manuscript I express grateful thanks to Andrew Pattison and Steve Martin.

INTRODUCTION

'Two old cousins of mother came from Leicester, two old maids. They were teachers during the war and when the air-raid siren went they went to sit under the stairs. I remember them telling my father "Oh, we were quite all right, Leslie, we put a tin bath over our heads!"'

'Old Ted used to wear sacks round himself, tied round with binder twine. My brother Edwin had said he should live on the farm or he'd have to go to Scarsdale Workhouse. Edwin always shared his sweet ration with him.'

'Women would receive a letter from the company, offering their profound regrets on the death of their husband at the pit, and enclosed in the same envelope was a notice to quit the company's house. That was the Bolsover Colliery Company. They were wicked to work for.'

Just three recollections snatched at random from the memories of Bolsover people featured in this collection. The last two reflect the very real threat of poverty and indeed destitution which hung like an ever-present Sword of Damocles above the heads of working people before the advent of the post-war Welfare State. The wartime memory is so typical of that peculiar English phlegm which characterizes so many of the wartime recollections in these pages.

In publishing three previous collections of old photographs of Bolsover and its surrounding villages, I have been conscious that many of those which concentrate on community events, whether it be chapel bazaars, school pupils standing to attention and squinting at the camera or the colliery band playing around a rain-swept memorial on Armistice Day are not merely visual images. Speak to anyone in the photograph and out pour the memories of the event itself and similar ones over the years. This is, of course, not the dry facts of local history but the conjuring up of people, circumstances and the events themselves, some of which have passed into communal folk memory. The sort of 'Do you remember when...' recollection.

So, an obvious next step in local history recording was not conjuring up images through pictures but visual images through memories and recollections. The result is this collection of *Bolsover Voices*, helping to bring the past to life. This 'past' ranges from people in their nineties who clearly remember, as adolescents, buses of cheerful young men setting off to Chesterfield in order to sign up for Kitchener's Army and the trenches of the Somme battlefields, through to the 1980s and the pit strike which was such a watershed in coalfield life. This also is now history and recollections of it are some of the profoundest in the collection.

The cross-section of people recorded is wide, ranging from the miner telling of the pit buttymen who had to be bribed to give work to the unemployed during the years of the Depression, to those sons and daughters of the professional and managerial classes recapturing a world of castle tennis club parties and dances held by the Duke And Duchess of Portland at Welbeck Abbey. There are memories of farmers, schoolteachers, miners, local

7

government workers, shopkeepers, housewives, businessmen and women.

Perhaps one of the most striking and fascinating aspects of Bolsover life is its combination of industrial and agricultural life. Scratch a little way beneath mining life and you come to that earlier farming existence. The pit itself provided employment to its male members but there was a deeper and longer established way of life on the land, usually one's own. So many memories are agricultural ones. The annual slaughtering of the pig, its chopping and salting to provide meat for the following year is a repeated memory. The threshing and harvesting, when the great threshing machines would crash their ponderous way between farms, when all the family put in a twelve-hour day and even the youngest would finish off with rabbit- and rat-catching as the corn was cut and vermin emerged. The expanding pit settlements provided a ready market for local farms, especially milk production, and Bessie Holmes, Ellen Spray and Jack Elliot recall delivering milk door to door, loading the unpasteurized and untreated liquid from cans into earthenware jugs.

Many of these agricultural recollections echo a much earlier world than that of the early and mid-twentieth century. Hawkers and gypsies travelling the rural backwaters of Scarcliffe and Palterton selling haberdashery or entertaining a few villagers on the green recall a tradition stretching back to the Middle Ages.

In the final years of the twentieth century we speak with surprise that in this electronic age no longer will the younger generation have a 'job for life'.

Yet this is not a new phenomenon. These memories remind us that before the Second World War few working people could feel secure about their employment prospects. Colliery companies recruited and laid off staff as trade demanded, farmers had good and lean years and paid work for agricultural workers was seasonal. Female teachers had to resign on marriage and tradespeople such as the Woodhouses and the Barfoots changed their type of business according to changes in community needs rather than those of fashion.

Recollections of domestic life are often the most vivid. Women (and it is always women) recalling wash days by hand, bread-making in a fireside oven, cooking for families of often between seven and eleven children in an over crowded two-bedroomed cottage where water was raised from a well in the yard and light depended on gas or even candle power was a feature for many. In some cases this held true right up to the 1950s. Photographs of nineteenth-century cottages might look idyllic but conditions inside were often hard physical drudgery.

It is this pace of change which makes it so relevant to record memories such as these before they vanish for ever. In some respects life in Bolsover, or indeed anywhere else, especially domestic life, did not change a great deal in the first fifty years of this century, or at least only superficially. Many of us as children in the 1950s lived in a house which with the exception of electricity and running water was not too dissimilar to the same house in 1910. For many there was still no washing machine, fridge, car, telephone, central heating or annual holidays. Change really began in the 1960s. The post-war boom, increased wages (although miners' wages were depressed until the mid 1970s), the demolition of slum property and the building of council estates, cheap foreign holidays and the availability of labour-saving devices in the home meant wholesale change in the way of life for the majority of people. As we approach the twenty-first century, to discuss with a youngster the early life of his father or grandfather elicits little understanding. Previous generations knew, because echoes of their grandparents' and even great-grandparents' world were all around them.

For every memory recorded here there are hundreds more, equally vivid, which lack of space prevented me from using. At the beginning of each interview I was always told by the interviewee that they had nothing of real interest to say. What in fact became apparent from the start of the recording cycle was that every one of us holds recollections of real interest to others. Some people were natural raconteurs. Others tell a story more simply. But what was so striking as the recording progressed was the plain and simple fact that none of us has a life devoid of interest. Our experiences count and are the warp and weft which help make sense of life and of how we relate to each other.

Personally, the editing of hours of recordings has been a fascinating undertaking. Through it all, the overriding impression has been one of hearing the voices themselves and when I read the transcriptions I can still hear those individual voices. Whenever possible I have retained the local dialect if used, individual phraseology and that unique flow of how individuals speak. Small changes have been made to some passages in order to clarify meaning to the reader, at the same time ensuring the absolute integrity of the recollection is given. Sadly, some of the interviewees have died since the recordings were made. This fact alone proves the relevance of the record itself. On countless occasions I was told that if only I'd spoken to late Uncle Jack or Aunt Gertrude before they had died, I would have been in for a real treat. In the same way, I've been told during twenty years of collecting old photographs of Bolsover that superb collections have been put on the back of the fire because on the death of Uncle Jack or Aunt Gertrude such photographs seemed worthless.

In *Bolsover Voices* I hope you can hear what I heard in talking to the people themselves. These verbal recollections are as much a part of our community's past as the visual images which illustrate them.

Bernard Haigh
Bolsover
1998

CHAPTER 1
Life at the Pit

Bolsover Colliery shortly before the outbreak of war in 1939.

A Job for Life

I left school in 1967 and went straight to the pit as an apprentice electrician. The day I signed I was told I'd got a job for life: 'You'll be here till you retire, young man.'

Ian Blakeley

Early Days at the Pit

My father was a Trade Union man but it had no strength, there was too much bribery. Fees were 6d a week and 3d for lads, which was a lot out of a small wage. We also paid 1s a week club money for doctors and hospitals and to the Miners' Convalescent Home at Skegness. The other four pits owned by Bolsover Company were Creswell, Crown Farm at Mansfield, Clipstone and Rufford. The Duke of Portland would allow no tips near Welbeck Abbey and Lord Saville at Rufford said there were to be no chimneys in view of Rufford Abbey.

The Spencer Union was formed in Nottinghamshire, a breakaway scab union who didn't like the politics of the miners' union. In 1911 we had a small local strike and the vicar, Webb Peplow, organized concerts in the national schools. Doctor Stratton played the piano and Miss Marsh at Town End could sing. I remember the strike of 1893 and they had to call the military out from Derby to Eastwood, it lasted sixteen weeks. In 1908 there was a further strike: eight hours' work, eight hours' sleep and eight bob a day, that's what they wanted. Shorter hours didn't come before the First World War.

Sir John P. Houfton was appointed manager of Bolsover Colliery in 1890, general manager in 1897 and a director of the company in 1910. He retained a seat on the board until his death in 1929.

Before the 1921 strike I was earning 3s 6d a day at the top and those at the coal face earned 6s a day. On the club you were paid 10s a week plus 7s 6d with your 'Lloyd George' (pension). There were two clubs, one for those down at the coal face who could afford to pay more each week and another for those at the pit top.

Holidays were Christmas Day, Whit Monday and Good Friday, all without pay. I was once threatened for wanting Bolsover Flower Day off, in August. We got our first one week's paid holiday in 1936; Bolsover Ambulance Division

Emerson Bainbridge, founder of the Bolsover Colliery Company and an original director.

were allowed to go to camp without pay for one week a year. I remember my mother dreading Easter because that was Friday off in one week and Monday the next.

In the period up to Christmas the pits often stood still because there was fog at the ports and they could not get rid of the coal. During the Depression there was no absolute unemployment in the pits, just bad trade. When Manny Shinwell was Minister for Mines he said that if all the companies were as good as Bolsover they would not need national-ization. They paid 6d or 1s a day more than Markham or Glapwell.

Before they built the villas in 1894 there was a canteen for the navvies and

colliers who were building the Model Village. Before the colliery schools were built the Institute was used as a school. The Co-op was leased to the Co-op movement by the Company.

The day I was twelve years of age my father said: 'Bill, you won't be going to school, tomorrow you start work.' I did cry. I got 4s a week for a twelve-hour day at the Co-op in the Model Village. We had to weigh everything: you got four Beecham's pills for a penny, a packet of Epsom salts for half a penny, carbolic soap was threehalfpence a pound, Colliers' bacon 6d a pound and sugar 2d a pound.

Every stall at the pit had a number and every tub for that stall had the same one. There were two weighmen, one for the company and the other for the men. He was paid out of union subs so the Company couldn't get at him. Agreement had to be reached by the weighmen for payment to the men.

You had to provide your own tools, picks and blades, drills and hammers, but not shovels or forks. A corporal in the pit was in charge of the lads.

Before the days of pit-head baths the company said they would allow you one ton of coal a month but you should fill twenty-one hundredweight for each ton. It was a good market for both sides and the coal came to each house on the tub railway. No women were ever employed at Bolsover, not even in the offices in the early days.

The Ambulance Room in the pit yard was equipped by the company although up until 1920 it was just a room in which to place the injured miners while they waited for the horse and trap to take them to Chesterfield hospital. There was also the Midland Miners'

In Memoriam

MARKHAM COLLIERY DISASTER, MAY 10TH, 1938.

THE TOLL OF THE MINES

'Twas not to the sound of rumbling drums,
To martial music or booming guns,
But far away from the seat of war
Almost in sight of their cottage door,
In the fight for existence, their daily bread,
And "the price"—nearly eighty heroic dead.
A sheet of flame, a sudden roar—
And gas-filled eddies, swept the floor,
And those of the living were maimed and torn
On that bright and sunny but tragic morn.

Rescuers came with devotion divine,
For duty comes first in the creed of the mine,
Tradition that's steeped in their bones and their breed,
And it comes to the top in the hour of need,
What daring supreme, can the mind linger on,
And they never give up hope till the last hope is gone,
In the search for a brother or father may be
To find them alone in Eternity.

No pen that exists can portray the scene,
Whatever we do or what might have been,
As doctors and helpers toiled on till they fell
To rescue them from this inferno of hell,
Who knew in what second as they too descend
Another explosion, and with it the end ?
And those of the injured thanked God, so they say,
To see once again the light of the day.

In Staveley, Duckmanton, Poolsbrook and Clowne,
There are hearts with sorrow and anguish bowed down,
For never again will the village street,
Echo to sounds of their tramping feet,
Or kiddies, O God, what a tragic sight,
Would go to meet Daddy on Friday night
For the pennies he earned, for his girl or his boy,
And the pleasure he got at the sight of their joy,
Or mothers, who waited at home by the door,
For the sight of the face they will see nevermore.

So if in your pity and anguish you feel
You would just like to help—it's to you we appeal,
It's a national debt that we can't put aside,
When we think of the way these breadwinners died
To get your black diamonds—that are paid for in blood,
Just risking their all for a livelihood—
That the fires might burn, though they that are gone,
And the wheel still turns, the world carries on.
By helping those left in these moments divine,
You will help just as surely those Sons of the Mine
By sending your money, it's the least you can give
To those who have died—that others might live.

Mrs. A. Gambling, 52, Mount Castle Street, Newbold Moor, Chesterfield.

Price - One Penny.

All profits to be given to the Mayor of Chesterfield's Markham Disaster Fund.

Disasters at the pit were the scourge of all mining districts and Markham was no exception. Major accidents occurred here in 1938 and 1973.

13

Underground haulage to the work face, 1939.

Underground loading point, 1939.

Fatal Accident Committee to which we paid one penny per week which paid out 7s 6d each week to widows whose husbands had been killed.

There was the Central line which went from Bolsover to Arkwright and then in a big loop to Heath and out to Nottingham. On Saturday nights they charged two bob for a special excursion – shopping and to the theatre to Nottingham. The 'Paddy Mail' went from Sheepbridge to Glapwell, calling at all stations.

Men at Bolsover Colliery travelled by the Paddy Mail but if there was a fog and it didn't turn up Bolsover pit couldn't turn, so Carr Vale Village was built to house miners and the station at Carr Vale opened in 1908. The land was owned by Earl Bathurst and before the village was built there was no such place as Carr Vale.

William Spray and Bob Banner
(recorded 1972)

A Good Fist

When I went back to t'pit I went into clerical side and I was there ten or eleven years until I applied for a transfer into t'stores. This clerical job was called 'making decorations'. It was in the weigh office and I had to improve my writing and arithmetic – and I did. They told me I'd got a 'good fist' – that's what they used to call it, and I kept that job for twenty-four years, until I retired at sixty-four and I was given a bottle of stout as a leaving present.

Alf Bentley

Alf Bentley beats the drum for Bolsover Silver Band.

John Plowright Houfton

Grandfather started life as a mining engineer. His father was manager at Micklefield colliery in Yorkshire and before that Moor Green, near Eastwood in Nottingham, where he went to school. Grandmother came from Garforth near Leeds. They met through the Wesleyan Chapel. They were both interested in music and he played the chapel organ. One of grandfather's brothers lived at Wellow House and another at Papplewick Hall in Nottinghamshire. I suppose you would call them *nouveau riche* today.

I remember Edwinstowe Hall which was the Bolsover Colliery Company's

15

Loading coal onto the face conveyors, 1939.

social centre for the miners and their families. In 1926 my brother and sister and I went to stay at Mansfield with our grandparents and grandfather was presenting the prizes at the pit boys' sports. He was a terrific orator and kept banging the table. The cups were going up and down and the children were really impressed.

Grandfather was a Liberal in politics but he turned Conservative in order to get a seat. I remember during the 1926 strike there was a miners' leader called Cooke who said my grandfather should be dusted down and put on a shelf which at the time I thought was an awful thing to say. I remember going to Parliament to hear him present his maiden speech. He also became Mayor of Mansfield and Sheriff of Nottingham which the children thought was really amusing. After Bolsover they moved to

Carr Bank, Mansfield which is now a hotel. I think the house was owned by the Duke of Portland.

The servants had their own floor with a separate chauffeur's house, a lodge for the gamekeeper and houses for the two gardeners. Some of grandfather's income came from shares in the Bolsover Jam Company.

My grandmother was older than Grandpa. She died just before the last war, aged eighty-seven, outliving him and my mother.

Jean Page

Eviction

Women would receive a letter from the company offering their profound regrets on the death of their

Bolsover Colliery sidings with loaded wagons ready for dispatch, 1939.

husband at the pit and enclosed in the same envelope was a notice to quit the company's house. That was the Bolsover Colliery Company. They were wicked to work for.

Pete Jones

The 1984 Strike

I was Training Officer and in COSI which was a branch of the NUM, so I worked through the strike.

Throughout the strike St John's entered national competitions, as in other years, and I had to get passes from the NUM secretary at Bolsover Colliery to enable members to get through the pickets and practise in the St John's HQ.

Roy Madin

Union Split

Unions and management were probably better at Bolsover than at any other pit in the area. After the strike this altered as you had two unions involved, the NUM and the UDM. This was a bit of a rarity, because Bolsover was a Derbyshire pit with a Nottinghamshire Union and the membership was half and half. After

Bolsover Colliery in the late 1970s.

1985 that caused some conflicts, but generally, for production, it was quite unified.

Ian Blakeley

Village Bobby

The village bobby [at New Bolsover] lived across the street. One in particular was called Bobby Suggs and at one time when I'd got my arm in a sling in a pot I couldn't do anything and it came time for t'allowance coal. The lorry was Jim Blood's. He lived on Hill Top and one day he brought the lorry round when t'wife was at work. He tipped the coal and I thought I'd have a go at getting it into the coal house with a bucket. Usually I'd use a barrow. Bobby Suggs came across: 'What are you doing out?' he called, so I said 'It's this coal, it wants shifting.' Well, he was a big powerful chap with a moustache. He took off his cape, borrowed the barrow and shovelled it in. Swept up and everything! Some of the other bobbies were a bit on t'management side and were out for everything they could get. I remember at one time my granddad lived at Meadow Bank and I asked Whiting, on Castle Lane, who had a fruiterer's shop, if they would take some of our coal to granddad's on their dray, because he hadn't got any. Anyway, they did and put the bags in granddad's coal house. Anyway, the next day, pit manager wanted to see me. 'Bentley,' he said, this was Hesketh, 'I hear you've been selling coal.' I said no. 'Are you calling me a liar?' he says. 'No,' says I. 'I gave it to my old granddad. He's a pensioner and hasn't got any.' 'Well, you

18

should have forfeited it if you had too much,' said Hesketh. So he punished me by docking my next load, so I daren't do it anymore.

Alf Bentley

A Hard Life

Life was hard for miners. A miner living at Bolsover and working at Oxcroft would walk or cycle to work and probably be told, 'We don't need you today, off you go.' They wouldn't receive a penny. I remember the 1926 strike. Up on the wall near us on Hill Top was written the word 'Blackleg' and I hadn't a clue what a Blackleg was. Miners went through a terrible time then. At school my father ran a soup kitchen with the staff and I remembered being very annoyed because I wasn't a miner's child!

Joyce Leaning

Tub Railway

The tub road used to run around the village. There were tubs which used to turn over; there was a catch at t'side and it emptied t'contents and tipped it into the opening. Allowance coal it was called.

Alf Bentley

The 1926 Strike

My dad worked in the wages department at the colliery offices and during the strike dad, of course, being one of the officials, was working and I can remember going home one night and during the night they'd been and put black gas tar crosses on the windows because he was working. There wasn't any trouble in the streets but I remember getting into trouble with my mother during the strike because at the butcher's they were giving soup away but we didn't have it because my father was working. One day I was coming home from school and some boy I used to play with; we used to play in the road in those days; kick-can and those sorts of games, and this lad was coming out and spilling his soup. Of course, me, I said, 'I'll carry it for you,' so I did, and they lived over the way from my mother. When I went in she said 'What have you got on your frock?' and I said 'Oh, I've been helping Stan to carry his soup.' Well, she didn't half get on to me; 'People will think it's for us and it isn't.'

A.W.

Poverty

I remember a charity coming round with boxes of second hand children's shoes and they would find a pair for all those without. Grandfather would come home in his pit dirt before the days of pit baths. He stripped off in the living room and his clothes were put on the line to be dressed down with a carpet beater.

Pete Jones

Bolsover Colliery officials outside the offices in the early days of the company in the 1890s.

Accident at the Pit

They were setting people on at Ramcroft Pit, my mother went up with me and I got a job for seven or eight weeks. The point was I was earning a copper or two for my mother. Then, when that packed up I got a job at Bolsover Pit on the screens and I lasted there about six months. Then I was on the dole but I got fed up with this lack of money and although I didn't want to go down the pit there was little choice.

We had bottles, not a Dudley, and no helmet or boots, you went in caps and even slippers. Sometimes I got fourteen shifts in and bought 18s home. We were in this house then, this would be in the 1920s. I was what you call a greaser, we had to make sure that the trucks were running properly. One shift my hand got caught in t'rope and it got me fast in t'wheel and it's amazing it didn't pull it

off. I can remember it now as if it were yesterday. I shouted and squealed and they stopped t'rope and pulled me out. I had to hold it on, I didn't want to lose a hand. Bolsover Colliery only had one ambulance at the time and took me Chesterfield Hospital. I was in seven weeks and three days. The wife was working at Ryland Works earning a bob or two, wages were very low. There was nothing in this room, just a table and chairs in t'kitchen, and a bed upstairs.

The compensation I got was 30s and out of that was taken heat and light and rent, so we had 14s a week to live on.

Alf Bentley

Uncle Horace

Horace Tinsley was a bit of a rum lad. If you upset him he'd start to cry tears of anger and rage, and if he did you had to keep your head down because he'd turn nasty. After the 1926 strike they held a vote whether or not to go back to the pits. Father and Horace voted to return. Horace always had a pint of beer at the Cavendish on his way home. One day he went in and didn't half get some stick about being a blackleg and scab, until tears were falling down his cheeks. He drank his beer, walked out and went to the toilet in the pub yard. He was followed with taunts. So, when he came out he knocked his tormentor down, picked him up again and rubbed his face up and down the stone wall. It was like a butcher's shop. The next day when he went to the Cavendish for a pint no one said a word. He was the only man in Bolsover who could throw a stone over the viaduct. A chap called Fred Thompson had a shop on the corner where the library now is, and he reckoned he could throw better than Horace. So, a week's wage packet was put on it. They could each choose three stones to their liking and it was the best of three throws. Fred's first went straight over. His second one dropped on the line and a third came back. Horace got three straight over so he took Fred Thompson's week's wages.

Normally, if a tub came off the rails at the pit it took four men to put it back. Horace did it on his own. One day, after doing this he went home with a headache and died the next day with a cerebral haemorrhage.

John Tinsley

Farm Pub

My brother worked at the pit, but not down the pit, on the property side. He slated all those houses at Creswell village. He brought a motorbike to get to Creswell but he wanted more money so he took the pub at Scarcliffe, the Horse and Groom which was a farm and a pub. We stayed three years and the farm paid but the pub didn't. When they put beer up to 6d a pint we didn't have any customers for two or three days after that.

The miners at the time were working at Glapwell. They walked there every day and when they got there the management would say 'We'll have you, you and you, the rest come back tomorrow.'

Bessie Holmes

Two Strikes

After the 1972 strike things were different to 1984. The earlier one was solid and when we went back there was unity. In 1985 things weren't the same because the men were split and it caused such division. I worked at the beginning then came out and went back before the end. The feeling ran very deep; I know of families which are still split and perhaps always will be forever.

Ian Blakeley

Pit Pony Races

The pit ponies had stables at the pit and once a year they brought them into the field where that tip is now. A beautiful meadow it was, with little streams running through it. Once a year, in summer there was a fête and we had pit pony races. All the jockeys are dead now – oh bar one, a chap up Bolsover, he'll be ninety-two now. His name was Cain Ogden. They'd roll a circuit and have races, right the way through Saturday afternoon. And all the horse manure was free. You could have as much as you wanted, so long as you carted it away.

Alf Bentley

A Living Thing

Conditions down the pit did improve. A pit is a live thing, it's mother nature, isn't it? You couldn't expect it to be the same from one day to the next as things shifted.

Roy Madin

The Butty System

My father moved to Bolsover when Bolsover pit first started to mine coal, in 1891. That's when they got down to the top hard seam, a good seam that went 356 yards down. He came from Huthwaite for better prospects. Often men came from Langley Mill and Moor Green in Nottinghamshire where seams were much thinner. Some came because they were cricketers and Bolsover Colliery had a good club!

The stallmen or the buttymen made a lot of money. Two or three men were put in charge of a stall, which is a

section of coal about eighty yards long with a runner road in the middle, thirty to forty yards each side. The buttyman was really a foreman in sole charge of this section of coal, under the pit deputy. He had a contract and paid the men what he liked, usually a pittance. A buttyman got his job with how much he could tip the undermanager, or he was a cricketer or footballer and played for the colliery company team! The stall comprised of gettars and pillars and the buttyman or stallman got 1s for every tub of coal they turned out. Bolsover colliery was then turning out three thousand tons a day. They also paid the Duke of Portland 6d a ton, that was his perk for all the pits on his land. Coal is the same as wood, it has a grain, so if you work at the edge of the pit you are working against the grain, but at the face with it, which is easier. Some men had a better stall than others, but they paid the undermanager for it. The butty system stopped with modernization in the 1930s when the coal was put on to belts and you didn't need a butty as a foreman. In 1906 the buttyman took home £20 a week while the coal face worker was lucky if he got 7s 6d a day. The buttymen lived in a Model Village until they built their own houses on Castle Lane or up Station Road.

William Spray and Bob Banner
(Recorded in 1972)

Fairness

When the Bolsover Colliery was a private company no-one was promoted from the ranks. After nation-alization there were managers and under-managers with little education but who went to night school to learn the trade. Before that it was university people from outside and the sons of colliery owners. After vesting day people with ability were offered jobs of responsibility. However, the private company were good on mechanization. They were among the first to have underground conveyers and pit-head baths. But it was all for profit, not particularly to improve the conditions for the workers.

The butty system was a type of subcontracting. Each buttyman had a gang working for him and they paid the men in that gang what they thought they were worth or what they could get away with. There was bribery and corruption. Men would give the buttymen an orange with a gold sovereign under the skin. It was a way of buying work for the day or the next week.

Pete Jones

Colliery Brickyard

The top hard seam coal was glorious, beautiful coal. The colliery would make all its own bricks. They carted all the clay from the clay hole to the brickyard.

By the football field there used to be a rope from t'pit. I had a granddad who worked in t'brickyard in t'engine house and the rope used to come up t'side of t'railway. There was another bridge down there and t'rope used to come down this football pitch which was the clay hole. My granddad was t'foreman then. I used to go down and see him.

There were two brick presses and all this clay was taken down to t'pit to make the bricks.

Alf Bentley

The Colliery Manager's Family

I imagine my grandmother, as wife of the colliery manager, played a big part in the social life of Bolsover. I really knew them after they moved to the Mansfield colliery which was also owned by the Bolsover Company. Here she was very active in the Methodist chapel and the district hospitals. Today, I suppose you would call her a great do-gooder, but it was in the nicest possible way. Grandpa was such a busy person it was good that she was also busy in her own right. She didn't just stay at home and do nothing.

I remember the servants my grandparents had. They had four maids and they always came from Bolsover. They were absolutely super people. There were two sisters, I remember, Ada and Daisy. One of them married a Mr Hare who ran the swimming baths at Mansfield where I learnt to swim. Their cooking was absolutely super. Grandmother was a Yorkshirewoman and she obviously taught them how to cook, although in those days she didn't do anything in the house. She always said she had a light hand with the pastry, although I can't imagine her in the kitchen. They were lovely people and had a marvellous relationship with their servants. The gardener Gilbert also came from Bolsover and he always had Grandpa's cast-off clothes so he looked very neat and tidy. Baker the chauffeur, who was a great character, married one of the cooks at my great uncle's house.

Jean Page

Qualifications

If you were a good sportsman and a good bandsman you couldn't go wrong with Bolsover Colliery Company.

Pete Jones

Family Pit

Bolsover colliery was a 'family pit'. It was a small town and all the local workforce went to Bolsover. Whereas Markham Pit was more cosmopolitan; they came from all over, as locally there was only Duckmanton and it was a large pit. I think family pits worked better.

Roy Madin

Nationalization

Nationalization was seen as an exciting time for mines. I think the miners thought that after being under the heel of the coal owners for so long they would be running the collieries, but it was really the same people with different titles.

Don Bateman

Beer Ration

The villas were lived in by under-managers and overmen, but mainly the 'big noises' at Area Office. At the first house I used to cut his hair for him. He eventually died, a big whisky drinker, that's what killed him eventually. Bramfitt he was called, Chief Surveyor of Bolsover Colliery Company. I got on well with him, in fact he's been in this room, but he used to like his whisky. Every night he was down at the Welfare. Before the club officially opened he was sat in t'best room with t'steward and he'd collar me to have a drink with him. I detested the stuff but drank it to suit him. The officials lived in t'villas and the cottages were for miners – lesser people.

When you drank beer in the Welfare you could only drink so much and if you were working the orders came from management that you mustn't touch any beer prior to going to work. I remember them words! And even if you were on days and went in at nights for a drink you were more or less warned – not too much!

Alf Bentley

The End of the Pit

When the pit closed it was a traumatic experience. I had six months when I'd fall out with my shadow, but you had to vent your feelings. You do get over it, but some people took it much harder than others. Some didn't find it easy, didn't move on. Others are still out of work, fourteen years later. It was a terrible time but I

Bolsover St John Ambulance Brigade winners, 1969. They are, from left to right: David Nunnery, Malcolm Spencer, Martin Bust, Roy Madin, Norman Bust, Bill Broughton. The trophies include NCB National Finals Cup, Thorneycroft Trophy and the Area Coal Board Trophy.

think most people moved on. Some are very resilient and miners are strong in this respect. It's a part of our lives which has gone now. You have to move on.

Ian Blakeley

Co-operation

Even through the 1984 strike when we had St John's members in the NUM and the UDM there was no bitterness in the HQ when they were practising together. There had to be no politics in the SJAB.

Roy Madin

'Full of Hypocrisy'

My father was a local preacher and president of Bolsover Miners' Union which was affiliated to the Derbyshire Miners' Union, which in its turn affiliated to the National Miners' Association. Enoch Overton was the secretary of the union, and another big man at 'prims'.

The men were pressed to go to chapel by the colliery company. The management went so you were expected also to attend. The place was full of hypocrisy.

When I came to Bolsover in the early 1890s there was the Primitive Methodist chapel in Cotton Street.

Roy Madin, Paul Kelly and Ian Blakeley, with actor Windsor Davies and the Hinkstone Rose Bowl, 1991.

Town End chapel and the Wesleyans on Hill Top weren't built. The new Congregational church on Castle Street wasn't built, just the old chapel on High Street.

The Catholics worshipped in a hut off High Street and the Salvation Army met in a hut on the Back Hills, later moving to Cotton Street when the Prims built the Town End Chapel.

The Town was Liberal because the manager of the colliery, Houfton, was Liberal. The council was a mixed bunch before 1926. Merrill Stubbins was an undertaker, William Day a headmaster, John Henry Adsetts a publican. Others included Mr McKay and Mr Streets. All were independent.

William Spray (recorded 1972)

Colliery Farm

They kept the big shire horses there, for pulling coal wagons. There were also pigs, sheep and cows and wheat was stored there. When they were thrashing I've helped to catch rats. I can remember them now, the big corn stacks were full of vermin.

Alf Bentley

A Local Tyrant

The officials at the colliery saw it differently from the miners. My grandfather used to get up at four o'clock, walk to the colliery, reach the pit bottom and the buttymen would go round picking them out like slaves. 'You, you and you and the rest can go home.' I remember my mother saying that as a child she would wait for him to come home workless and ask for his jam sandwiches.

The colliery company literally ruled your life. If the manager was a tyrant then everyone was in fear of him. Hesketh was hated. He daren't go out at night without a stick and a dog, he was so disliked.

Pete Jones

New Bolsover Colliery Village

The village was beautiful in those days. There were rose gardens and seats on the Green and Bolsover Colliery farm land opposite. You could leave t'back doors open and take an armchair on to t'green. We came in 1937. In the village in those days you had to look after your house and garden and you had to adhere to the rules, otherwise out! And when they said that, it meant out! You didn't ask any questions. I have heard of people being evicted, quite a few of them. They were very severe.

The Green was beautiful; rose trees, laurel trees, it was really beautiful. There was a groundsman and if he saw you he used to run after you. He was at it every day. He also had a bowling green and a cricket field to look after.

Alf Bentley

Modern Mining Methods

When I first started working at the pit we were mining 30,000 tons of coal a week, using 1,400 men which made 18,000 saleable tons. Twenty years

Electricians at the Colliery in the 1930s. Albert Leaning is fourth from the left. Nothing is known about the occassion.

later they were mining out the same amount with 400 men. Mechanization meant thirty-six men at the coal face went down to eighteen and with more production.

Mechanization made coal production faster but the teams became smaller so you had to do more. I suppose it was easier than pick and shovel but the machines moved faster. Even in the 1980s I remember we had a man at the pit who always seemed to be using a pick and shovel at the coal face. Towards the end we worked on the idea that as the machine comes to the end of the face anyway let it cut the face itself out.

Ian Blakeley

Bolsover Colliery as it was in 1889.

The Under-Manager

This house on Shuttlewood Road was built for an under-manager at the colliery and father bought it in 1902. Next door was the home of Tylden Wright, a director of the colliery company and the one next door to that was the cottage where his valet lived.

Kath Palmer

John Plowright Houfton

When my grandparents, John Plowright Houfton, who was the first colliery manager, and his wife, Frances, left Bolsover they were presented with a large amount of silver. Not just from the colliery people but from friends also. It included a silver tray, cake stands; a tremendous amount, which today my son has. A few years ago he had the tray repolished in Leicester and the polisher asked where the rest of the set was. Upon being told that it was now spread around the family, he said that he had been an apprentice at Mappin and Webb in Sheffield when it was commissioned.

My grandfather's family all grew up in Bolsover and the two daughters, one of whom was my mother, went to school at Queen Elizabeth's School in Mansfield. They had to travel by train from Bolsover and were weekly boarders. They both did well. One went to the Slade School of Art and the other daughter, May, to the Royal Academy of Music. The sons attended the Leys School, Cambridge, and trained as engineers. Then the First World War broke out and the eldest was killed. The youngest son didn't do very much career-wise but he did fight in both wars.

Jean Page

Peter Thelwall and Jean Page, grandchildren of Sir John Plowright Houfton, outside Bainbridge Hall, 1998.

'You Lost All Sense of Time'

I started at Bolsover Pit as a bricklayer's labourer, but that didn't last long. When you got a job in the pit you had to be prepared to do anything, whatever the manager wanted. I don't really like to go back to those days; they were tough, terrible days, very dangerous, when at times the pit roof was almost on your head. Many's the time, even now I've retired, when I think of all that rock above you, it makes your belly ache to think about it. But human life in them days was cheap.

The manager when I was working at the pit was Hesketh, a man with a moustache and a dominating voice; it penetrated you and I hated him, his voice fair drilled into you, although in some ways I got on with him. On number one shaft we were sinking from the Top Hard to Waterloo and sinking another pit bottom. We were on a twelve-hour night shift seven days a week and I was courting. I only had three hours to sleep during t'day and I couldn't see my wife during the week as she worked days, so we only saw each other once a week. Once you were down t'pit you lost all sense of time.

Alf Bentley

CHAPTER 2
Leisure Time

On his retirement, Bruce Woodcock, Heavyweight Boxing Champion, became the landlord of the Anchor. He is seen here joining in Coronation festivities in 1953. Woodcock retired from boxing in 1950 and died in 1997.

Community Working

I joined the WI and the Mothers' Union, followed by Dr Barnardo's, and we later formed the lifeboat committee in 1966. The organization said it was the fastest formed committee they'd ever known. Sheila Bagguley, Mrs Phipps, all the people who are already doing things can usually find time for others. We decided to have a big do each year and as Dr Hughes, who was a churchwarden, was on the committee we were able to get the church hall for nothing. We had a cockerel which we stood in a cage on the raffle prize stand. Young Dr Lane was president and when he gave a speech this cockerel started up; it was the funniest thing! Anyway, the person who won didn't want it so Joe Mason took it and it lived in his house, with its own cushion and he became really fond of it. Then we held a French night including can-can dancers from Chesterfield School. The lifeboat committee also did the first cheese and wine evening in Bolsover and it went down a bomb, then everyone jumped on the bandwagon. We had hoedowns in Spray's barn at Palterton and dinner dances at the Sportsdrome. Charles was very involved with the British Legion and I became president of the ladies' section. At the start we still had people who had fought in the First World War and we had dug-out suppers where you pretended you were in the trenches! Well, of course we didn't have trenches in the second war so we introduced another way of making money. We also ran the poppy appeal and I was on the county committee of the WI which took a lot of time.

Bunty Margerrison

Sportsdrome Beginnings

The Sportsdrome started life as a gym when some local men were interested in boxing. Five years later it became licensed and grew so that eventually it had bars, a restaurant and dance floors. For some reason when it was a boxing gym some Tongans who were interested in the sport came and settled here and on one occasion Queen Salote of Tonga paid a visit. When Bruce Woodcock, the boxer, came he took over as licensee of the Angel and trained in the gym.

Anne Woodhouse

St John Ambulance Brigade

I started with St John Ambulance Brigade in 1962, press-ganged into it by Les Rimmer. They wanted someone for the competition team and I went down to the village hall thinking I shan't enjoy this. Well, I'm still coming thirty-six years later.

The St John's flourished when the pit was going strong and all colliery officials had to have a first aid certificate and the only way they could get it was through St John's. They met every Sunday for practice, or one of the local doctors would give a lecture. People thought that when the colliery closed we would also but we were determined that it wouldn't. The building we are in now was in the colliery yard and we moved it here to Hillstown.

Roy Madin

Hill Top tennis courts before the First World War.

Boys' Brigade

The colliery ran the Boys' and Girls' Brigades. They used to do their drills and things in the Colliery Schools in the evenings, and use the Green. The Boys' Brigade was a bit like St John's, almost like a training for the army: drill, gymnastics and a camp near Skegness every year. There was a uniform and a musical instrument to play, a kettle drum or bugle.

Ken Leaning

Mixed Doubles

My aunt played bridge with Dr Stratton's wife, Mrs Bradshaw, who owned a house set back on Cotton Street which is now the 'Linen Box', and Mrs Cox, who ran a private school from Heath House on High Street. All very ladylike it was!

My aunt Emily also played tennis, at courts off Hill Top, with Miss Adsetts from Sutherland Farm. Now, Miss Adsetts was 5ft 11in and tall and thin, rather like Edith Sitwell in appearance. Auntie Emily was 4ft 6in, small and round, so it must have been quite a sight.

Pam Ashley

Bolsover Feast

This was a wonderful, magical time. Huge coloured caravans rolled in and stalls were erected. These included a pea man and toffee which he chopped into bite-sized pieces. There was brandy snap and Bailey's roundabout which had to be hand cranked, dodgems, the cake walk, Proctor's Peacocks with a famous steam organ. The whole event was a cacophony of sound and one year I remember a man jumping from a tall tower with his clothes ablaze into a tank of water.

Much of the time we could see all this from our attic skylight as we overlooked Kitchen Croft. We stood on tables and peered across. It was a time like no other.

Betty Hunter

Carr Vale Cinema

The Central Hall and Charlesworth Street were all a built from local bricks. My husband's father built the cinema and the house next door below. It wasn't just a cinema, there were turns also and we used to go and meet them, these turns, from Chesterfield, on a lorry with their effects. They were singers, dancers, magicians, acrobats, that sort of thing, and we used to have find digs for them in Carr Vale. They had turns on between the films and I used to sit at the side of the wings and watch them. There was a pianist who played for the silent films; he was a nice man and he always had a trilby on.

Dorothy Cutts

Topping Up

One woman used to come to the back door of the pub and she would pass me a couple of empty bottles and say 'Fill these up, duck – and don't put them on the bar, my Mester's in there!'

Bessie Holmes

Fred Peters: Sportsman

There was a tennis club at the castle. My father and Kath Palmer were partners. There was a shop opposite where the Sportsdrome is now, Barfoot's, where they made wonderful ice cream and I used to have to fetch the ice cream for the strawberries. They would play all in whites when they had a match. Father used also to play cricket, golf at Tapton and eventually bowls. My mother said that all his life was spent running after a ball! We were even married at half past ten in the morning so that the men could all go the football match afterwards.

Marion Jones

Doe Lea

As children in the Model we would come out of Sunday School and go for a walk down Buttermilk Lane, over the fields to the Doe Lea where Coalite is now. Just green fields and the river: you could swim in the Doe Lea then.

Ken Leaning

Decazeville

I first went to Decazeville on an exchange in 1972. There was Rita and Fred Inns, Charles and Bunty Margerrison, Jack and Mrs Spray, Dick Davies, his wife and son. We stayed in a hotel, just a room, no breakfast, and we were invited out to a meal every day. You had to be careful; if you were invited out for lunch you had a small

Entente Cordiale. The Bolsover–Decazeville exchange in 1972. Don Bateman is fourth from the left on the back row and on his left are Bunty Margerrison and Fred Inns. On the front row on the right is Rita Inns. In the centre are Jack and Mirab Spray with Charles Margerrison to their right.

dinner the day before and if invited out for dinner a small lunch the same day! Anyway, one lunch we went to was at Maddo's. She lived with her mother and father in an old colliery house and of course she got the best china out. It was a hot day and the table was laden with food and wine and there was a bottle of ice cool water which Charles passed to Fred. Anyway, the glass bottle held so much condensation it slipped out of his hand, dropping on to one of Maddo's ten inch plates, smashing it to smithereens. After the meal we went home and held a council of war, agreeing that we had to replace that plate. First of all we had to retrieve the bits, so we agreed that Fred and Charles would go to the front door and engage

Maddo and her mother in conversation and my job was to skip round the back and look for the pieces of the plate. Fortunately I did so, on a stone ledge by the dustbin, so I put them in my pocket, gave the signal to the others and returned to the hotel. In the town there was a shop which sold beautiful pottery, so we went, presented the pieces and asked for a replacement. The shopkeeper knew exactly where the original came from but he couldn't get a new one for some months, so we paid for it and he sent Maddo the plate when it was ready. She sent us a letter at Christmas, offering a 'thousand thanks' for the plate which had just arrived.

On that visit the council gave us a huge meal followed by drinks at the bar.

A view of Decazeville, Bolsover's twin town in France, as it was in 1969. Notice the colliery and slag heaps to the rear.

The wine was being lined up by the glass and one thing the French do on occasions like this is sing. So they started on songs of the Auvergne and I said to Charles 'We'll have to respond in kind.' He agreed, so he started on the 'Foggy Foggy Dew', he knew the words and I could manage the tune. We followed this with 'On Ilkley Moor Baht 'At'. The drinks kept lining up and I said to Charles 'They're going to drink us under the table.' 'Oh no they're not,' he said, 'Never mind Vive la France, Vive l'Angleterre!' Well, they gave up after a bit, and so did I. How were we going to get home, was my next worry. 'Never mind,' said Charles. 'The police here are appointed by the Mayor and we've got him with us!'

Well, the following day I wasn't too good and I had an appointment with the Chief Engineer to take me round this huge coal outcrop. We went in a little Citroën 2CV. Well, we bounced around this rough outcrop and there was the smell of wet coal in the hot weather, a horrible stench of sulphur and everything was covered in a blue haze. Going up and down in this car with a hangover was awful. We then went back to the house and more wine. What a day!

The French were so kind and hospitable, absolutely marvellous. One day we were walking by the newsagents when we saw a poster advertising a colliery disaster in England. It turned out to be at Markham, the 1973 pit cage disaster. So we immediately phoned home as some of our kids, fathers, and grandfathers and uncles could have been involved. The Coal Board confirmed the names of the dead miners and none of our kids had relatives involved, but it was a difficult homecoming.

Don Bateman

Turning the Coin

Where Martin's Travel is now lived a butcher, Arthur Shaw, and he and Fred Hunt were great friends. Every Tuesday night they would have a pipe and talk about their shares and the state of the markets. Well, one night about eight o'clock Arthur Shaw looked out of his window. 'Fred.' he says, 'you've got a ticket. What are you doing parking without lights? It's a minute past lighting up time and that new constable's walking around your car.' Fred sat back and said 'Well, in that case we'll have another pipe of baccy, Arthur.' So they sat down and at 8.30 Fred said. 'Is he still there, Arthur?' 'Yes,' was the reply. 'Well, let's go see what he says for himself,' says Fred. So, they went out and as they were walking up to the car the constable says 'Evening Sir, might this be your car?' 'Yes,' replied Fred. 'I have the honour of owning this fine piece of machinery. It's a Riley and I'm the only man in Bolsover with one.' 'Well,' says the constable, 'are you aware it's an offence to park it without lights?' 'Yes,' replied Fred, 'and I'm also aware that you've been walking around it for the past half hour and if there'd been an accident you would have been responsible for letting it happen. Instead of coming to find me and telling me, you ignored it.' 'Well, I didn't know whose car it was, and where

the owner was.' 'Come off it,' says Fred, 'anyone in Bolsover would have told you whose car it was and that always on a Tuesday night Fred Hunt and Arthur Shaw sit having a pipe of baccy. I think I will have to go and see Sergeant Burson about you. We can't have this sort of carry on.' The young constable stuttered, 'I hadn't realized it was like that, sir.' 'Well,' says Fred 'obviously you're new on the job, we'll forget all about this oversight. Good night, constable.' And he got in his car and drove off. The next morning at the police station Sergeant Burson heard the story and said to the new constable, 'Well, your education is complete now. I've been trying for years to give Fred Hunt a ticket and I've not succeeded yet!'

John Tinsley

Brass Bands

The brass bands were very good and of course every few miles there was another brass band, and now practically none at all. Bolsover Silver Prize Band used to play quite often in the castle grounds on a Sunday night. People would go and listen and youngsters would eye the opposite sex, it was a lovely atmosphere.

Ken Leaning

Bolsover Doctors

We were very friendly with the Gordon family on Oxcroft Lane. We had happy times round there. Dr

Gordon looked after mother. Kath Palmer used to go and we played tennis, although I was never up to their standard. They had their own tennis courts just beyond the terrace from the house.

At Anne Gordon's wedding there was a big marquee on the lawn. We went round for evening meals. Dr Gordon came to live in a house which belonged to us in the Old Market Place which is now Norman and Ludlums. Dr Spencer lived in the house and it became Kennington's the dentists. It was a big house with a music room at the back. Dr Spencer had three daughters, Violet, Marjorie and Dorothy, and two sons, all very musical. It was a beautiful house.

Ada Bagshaw

Charabancs

Oh, I was telling you about Wards and their charabanc. It had no top on it but we thought it was great. We hired it for the little chapel at Carr Vale. Mums, dads and kids, we all went to Skegness, a great treat that. They could convert it to a coal cart when it wasn't used as a charabanc.

A.W.

Amateur Operatics

My sister Ida attended the parish church where Mrs Paget, the vicar's wife, ran the Girls' Friendly Society. She was a very clever woman who instigated an amateur operatic society. Ida played the star lead in *The*

Young Bolsover gents. From left to right: Fred and George Hunt and Billy Shaw. The Hunts farmed the land off Moor Lane and George was famed as 'the best horseman in South Yorkshire, Nottinghamshire and Derbyshire.'

Country Girl which was held in 1933 in the church hall. She was also in *The Belle of New York*. There was great excitement at show time with dresses, rehearsals and make-up sessions. I was accused of secretly using her Pond's vanishing cream and Showfire hand cream which came in hard green blocks and set chapped hands and legs on fire, but after the first torture it did work. Sometimes I couldn't resist Ida's cheap perfumes but never understood how she knew.

I refused to go to Sunday school and hid behind the door on Whit Sunday

A production of *The Country Girl* in the church hall, 1933.

when chapels and churches paraded on Town End past our shop.

Betty Hunter

Family Affair

In some cases the St John's was a family affair: father would be in, sons followed and daughters and sisters would become nursing cadets. It is a very real tradition in mining areas.

Roy Madin

Lantern Shows

There were Saturday night magic lantern shows in the Assembly Hall and the collection was usually in aid of the heathen! Well, that didn't mean much to a child but it was fascinating. We had Felix the Cat cartoons in black and white on a flickering screen. It is a real memory, that.

I remember going to the Central Hall on a Saturday morning for the penny rush, and when we got older there were lovely dances at New Bolsover School or the baths where they put a floor over the pool. The Church Army Hut was for all the boys and young men in Bolsover. There were two billiard tables and you could sit round a fire and talk. On Sunday afternoons, we sat round and talked politics with Jack Spray and Jack Harrison. They were almost communist, they were: good people, believed in what they said, if a bit too earnest.

Joyce and Ken Leaning

Boys' Brigade

Now, the village hall, although it was a school, was the home of the

Bolsover Boys' Brigade band on the road to Winthorpe church, near Skegness in Lincolnshire, 1951.

Boys' Brigade and I was born and bred and ended up with the Boys' Brigade. I was a bugler and became a sergeant bugler until I had all my teeth out. Then I had to become the drummer and I kept that big drum right up to when the Boys' Brigade and Bolsover Silver Prize Band finished altogether and the drum went with them.

There was a Girls' Brigade, equally powerful, and St John Ambulance; all in t'Village Hall.

Alf Bentley

Jack Radford, the hunchback who ran it, his job seemed to be to keep everyone out. We did have dances in the Riding School, perhaps twice a year, but the floor was terrible and there was no proper lighting. The church hall was much better when the 'GFS', the Girls' Friendly Society, had a dance. Stan Cox's Band from Chesterfield, the Al Needham of former years, came. It was so posh, it was 2s 6d, atmosphere and everything!

Ken Leaning

Dances

The castle grounds were not really used for events; I don't know what the Portland family were thinking of.

Castle Bazaars

We used to hold church bazaars in the castle. The Duchess of Portland often came to open them and

39

An old folks' 'treat' in the Assembly Hall, 1948.

did a lot for Bolsover. I used to play golf at Welbeck Abbey; Mrs Paget, the vicar's wife, got us the permission. The colliery company organized a dance at Christmas in the underground ballroom in the Abbey. My brother and I won the spotdance prize and the Duchess presented us with a silver gravy boat. The Duke was a marvellous chap, very handsome. When the Duke and Duchess came to Bolsover they'd drive down by the school house onto the Terrace. Dad used to keep his sheep in the outer grounds of the castle. He slaughtered the sheep at the top of the back garden. The land stretched from Castle Street to High Street and he had a big slaughterhouse at the High Street end.

We played badminton at night in the Castle Riding School. Jack Radford, the custodian, let us do that. We had it lit by gas and played in our hats and gloves. In those days you could go in the castle any time so long as Mrs Radford let you. They lived upstairs in that part next to the Riding School and you could go onto the balcony and look down into the Riding School. She had a nice sitting room but it was ever so cold.

Kath Palmer.

Bolsover Cricket Club

In those days Bolsover Colliery Cricket Club team without exaggerating was just about county standard. The colliery used to advertise for somebody away,

Carr Vale Hotel bowling club, 1938.

usually from Yorkshire, who was a good cricketer, who could play in the team and also look after the ground and they really were a first class team. And they encouraged youngsters: so long as you kept off the middle square you could practise on the cricket field to your heart's content and it says a lot for the children that they did respect the rules without wrecking the hallowed turf in the middle.

Ken Leaning

Riding School Dance

My two sisters were in their twenties in the 1930s and went to all the Castle Riding School Dances. I loved their ballroom dresses and couldn't wait to grow up. When I did it was wartime and our clothes were on coupons. I always felt I must have missed out on something.

My sisters were both 'Hollywood-struck' and into Clarke Gable and waved hair. One played the piano and the other a banjo. We had musical evenings around the piano. I remember the Bolsover Carnival in 1933 and the Concert Party on the stage in the Riding School. My relative Billy Fern brought his ventriloquist dummy to entertain us.

Betty Hunter

Bolsover Society

The Bolsover Society started in 1970. Eric Bradley, Cliff Paulson and Ron Bladen were the original officers but they had no secretary so I volunteered and we had a meeting to formulate a

The New Bolsover Social Club were winners of the Clowne League darts and dominoes competitions in the 1950s. Alf Bentley (secretary) is in the centre.

programme. We invited members to subscribe to an annual programme and aimed for half a dozen concerts in the first year. We asked East Midlands Arts to help us financially but drew a negative response. They couldn't support us until we were established and we couldn't become established until we had some money. So, in the end we said 'sugar you' and organized a local concert with a guitarist and a quartet who sang close harmony and hill-billy songs. They cost us £50; the professional ones charged £500, which was out of this world to us. The Assembly Rooms had just a bare stage with no curtains, no backdrop, and on the night the quartet arrived, no guitarist. Anyway, after the halfway stage, he rolled up with this young lady in a miniskirt and started telling jokes which got bluer and bluer. He refused all calls to come off stage, but fortunately the jokes became so blue the kids couldn't understand them,

while everyone else was rolling in the aisles. In addition, the Assembly Rooms had formerly been a Methodist church and there was this arrangement that alcohol was not permitted. Anyway, this guitarist got hold of a glass of whisky. It was not turning out as we'd planned, but it did go off a treat.

Later, Jack Spray came round to see me and he said that he felt we ought to do this thing properly and have some curtains, backdrapes and spotlights. So he'd try and get the council to help, and they did. After the first year we aimed for ten or twelve concerts each year. We had championship brass bands, military bands, opera, piano solos, the lot.

On one occasion we had booked this excellent classical pianist and Eric Bradley was on stage announcing her, when he walked off and fell over clutching the curtains as he went. Fortunately they broke his fall. There was a deathly hush, everything fell silent, when he reappeared and announced his next trick!

We had a festival in 1973, floodlighting the castle, with tableau lights in Sherwood Lodge and ending up as dusk fell with a lone piper on the roof of the keep. We had two weeks of events and used Jack Spray's models for the illuminated shapes in Sherwood Lodge and built new ones. We got an epidiascope and projected a picture onto big sheets of hardboard, drew round it, cut them out and painted them.

Bolsover UDC were very helpful by providing the Assembly Rooms at a reasonable rate but the championship brass bands had to go down to the old colliery schools at New Bolsover. We would fill the Assembly Rooms with 300-plus people for some events. We had a base of subscribers of about 200 people and Cliff Paulson as publicity officer was very active in selling tickets.

We had Max Jaffa, his trio and his wife who sang; a brilliant night. The problem was money. East Midlands Arts did offer to underwrite one or two concerts but never offered hard cash. I had to hire grand pianos from Hofmeister at Brimington. Orchestras and Welsh choirs made things difficult because the stage wasn't big enough. However, Charles Margerrison helped with big boxes from the baths and they extended the stage by about a yard.

I was secretary of the Society for seven years, by which time interest was beginning to wane a bit and it only lasted a couple of years after that. It was a big job, secretary. Everyday I was doing something; ringing people up, writing confirmation letters and then on the day you just hoped that they'd turn up.

THE BOLSOVER SOCIETY

BAND

OF THE

RAF COLLEGE

CRANWELL

by permission of the Defence Council

Musical Director
Squadron Leader D. S. Stephens

SATURDAY, MARCH 23rd
VILLAGE HALL   1974
NEW BOLSOVER

A Bolsover Society programme for March 1974.

When Grimethorpe Colliery Band came they wanted to play Tchaikovsky's *1812 Overture* and needed two dustbins to use for explosives. So, we found two bins, emptied them round the back of the school and when the explosive went off, the rafters, which had accumulated eighty years' worth of dirt cascaded inches of dust onto the audience!

Don Bateman

Silver Prize Band

The band used to give some lovely concerts during the summer time. They used to play on t'green and we'd all take chairs out. It was grand and you

Bolsover Silver Prize Band marches through the Market Place on Remembrance Sunday in the 1940s.

could hear them up Bolsover. In a way of speaking if you were in t'band you got a good job. Put it like that they used to look after them. Oh, and we used to have dances and concerts galore. I used to play in the dance band. Eventually when I got older I used to play piano and electric Hawaiian guitar. I've played all over within a twenty-mile radius of Chesterfield.

Alf Bentley

Cinema

My first cinema memory was of the first 'talkie', Al Jolson in *Sunny Boy*. That would be about 1930. Later, I went to the Saturday twopenny rush at the Plaza. It was in at front and out at the back: noisy, steamy and fascinating.

Betty Hunter

The Sisterhood

My mother used to go the Sisterhood on Saturday night and one night she didn't come home until eleven o'clock and I said, 'Where have you been? The Sisterhood doesn't go on this long.' And she said, 'No, I didn't go. I met Mrs Gregory and she asked me to go with her to the dogs at Sheffield. I went out with only a bit of collection money but I won more at the dogs.' So that was mother's night out at the Sisterhood!

Bessie Holmes

Bolsover Feast

We used to have a musical festival every year in the castle grounds; a big stage with different choirs from all

Crowds attending the laying of the foundation stones, bearing the donors' names, for the Assembly Hall extension in 1909. Councillor Day is in the centre with his children – Les, Charles and Arthur – before him.

over the place competing. Bolsover Feast was on Kitchen Croft and on Sunday we had open air organ recitals. Hospital Sunday I think it was called.

A.W.

Duchess of Portland

I remember the Duchess of Portland opening the bowling green on the Hornscroft and I remember vividly she had an enamelled face.

Joyce Leaning

CHAPTER 3
Life on the Land

William Barfoot and his horse, Prince, in Castle Street before the First World War.

The old Market Place in the early years of the century. The gas lamp was replaced by the War Memorial in 1921. The bank, later Greenwood's chemist, is the only building no longer remaining, although the centre house and C.H. Mason's have been remodelled.

Harvest

Thrashing days were a nightmare really. They'd come with those big thrashing machines the night before, because they had to get the steam up early. The men would come in the house at 6.30 a.m. and eat really fat boiled bacon and huge pieces of bread, all home-made. They'd wash it down with a great big mug of hot sweet tea and get sorted. At 11 a.m. it would stop and we'd take a couple of cans of cocoa and a basket of mugs down the yard and they'd all have a mug of cocoa. At night the thrashing man and his helper would come in the house and have dinner with us; they were big, black and dirty. The days were of twelve hours or more. It was wonderful when the combine harvester came, but there was something about the thrashing machine though! You can hardly believe they travelled on roads and from farm to farm. They were so huge.

The corn went into three different bags: that only fit for fowls, then the better stuff and finally the best. The chaffman had to keep raking the chaff out from underneath to stop it getting blocked up. A terrible job that, he must have got it on his chest. People used to buy chaff for their horses to eat and for bedding as well. Harvesting was such a dirty job. Thrashing days were also rat-catching days. Menfolk and lads used to think it was lovely. They'd have their big sticks but the rats usually got away. We also kept six or eight cats to keep the vermin down.

Ellen Spray

Portland Family

There was a lot of unemployment after the First World War and men would go into the estate yard at Welbeck and ask for work. The Duke would get them to dig a trench twelve feet square and four feet deep, keeping the soil separate from the subsoil. If the estate manager was happy with the trench he would ask them to fill it in again. But you mustn't be able to tell the hole had been dug. The Duke's idea was that money should be earned not given. That way men would retain their self respect. He'd never let anyone starve, wouldn't the Duke. He'd always find work for anyone. The Portland family were cursed with having too few sons, and eventually the male line died out and the title with it. When my mother and father lived at Clipstone there was a girl, a cripple. The local doctors had done what they could and the Duchess of Portland asked if she could take her to see her own doctor in Harley Street. So, the chauffeur came, took her to Nottingham station and they travelled to London with the Duchess in attendance. An operation was paid for and accommodation at a nice medium-class hotel. When she was back home the Duchess would call regularly to see how the girl was progressing. I only remember seeing Duchess Winifred once. I think she used to use arsenic on her face to keep it white. She would come to open the Flower Show at the castle with this deathly white face.

John Tinsley

Florence Nightingale's Trap

In the stackyard at Mill Farm was Florence Nightingale's trap, a lovely high wheeled thing it was. Mr Holmes had bought it in a sale at Lea, near Matlock, which is where Florence Nightingale came from. When he built Lea Holme Estate on the Chesterfield road he put together Lea and his own name for the houses. Each house cost £450 and they were built by Jack Crowder, the local builder. The end house is built at an angle, where the access road for the whole estate was to be, but the war came and the only ones to be built were those on the main road.

Jack Elliot

Beginnings

My father came from Palterton. He was born just under the hill at what we used to call the White House. My mother came from Tibshelf. He went to be an apprentice joiner and my mother's father was an undertaker and that's how they met. They took up farming again but joinery was useful as he made all new doors for the house.

Ellen Spray

Castle Lane

Castle Lane, or Water Lane as it was called then, was a narrow lane with streams flowing down. John Henry Adsetts who kept the Angel public house grazed cows on the right hand side. The old Angel yard was a

The White House, Scarcliffe – and a petrol pump.

farmyard. The old Cavendish pub was called 'the Vaults' and Christopher Hinde farmed the Kitchen Croft.

Ethel Hodkin

Scarcliffe in the 1930s

Petrol in 1931 was 1s 1d a gallon. My father was an overseer at Sherwood Colliery and wanted to get out so he bought the White House at Scarcliffe and installed petrol pumps. Eventually he opened a general store. Scarcliffe in those days was very much an agricultural village with workers employed on two big farms, Wildgoose and Atkins, although most people at the top end of the village were mining families.

Norah Ley

Suicide

We had a man who committed suicide at the back of the cow shed. Old Ted, who used to come with the thrashing machine, was turned out at Stanfree and came to live in our cow shed. He used to wash himself in the cow trough and at night when the air raids were on and they were bombing Sheffield he woke us all up, he got frightened you know. Anyway, one Sunday morning one of the evacuees had taken his breakfast out and old Ted was waving his arms around – he'd cut his throat. We called the ambulance and the police and the policeman said, 'Now Ted, what's the matter with you?' and he turned round and the policeman could see all the mess. He walked out as white as a sheet. Old Ted was taken to Scarsdale hospital, where he died.

Bessie Holmes

William Barfoot Snr with Pat Mason, his granddaughter, in the fields fronting Castle Lane in the early 1920s.

Fruit Picking

We used to pick gooseberries at Tinsley's fields off Welbeck Road and filled huge buckets for 3d a bucket. The fruit went to the jam factory at Carr Vale. The first time I went abroad I financed the trip by strawberry picking at Tinsley's. I picked enough to get me to France, Italy and Switzerland on a motorbike.

Pam Ashley

Palterton in the 1920s

I was born in 1917 at Carr Farm, Palterton, under the hill, and we left and came up here when I was five to Palterton Hall. I was there for twenty years, when I got married and moved along the street. I married Charles Spray and lived there for twenty years when I moved back to the Hall.

Palterton was a farming village and those that weren't farming were mostly miners. There were also smallholdings and a small pig holding next door and most of the farmers kept a herd of cows. Three farmers hawked milk in the village and one, Mr Harrison, used to walk to Bolsover with his milk. We all had our own customers; you didn't encroach on your neighbours.

We've got the mission church in the village. The Vicar of Scarcliffe walked across to take Sunday school. He always wore a straw Yardley hat, winter and summer. The little mission was always full as they had big families in those days and it was nothing for three or four children from each family to attend Sunday school. We had to learn the Collect and on Sundays we weren't allowed to play. We could read a book or go out walking but not play at all. We daren't have touched a ball.

There were seven of us at the Hall and we seemed to fill it. In the kitchen all the deal tables and stone flagged floors had to be scrubbed. If there was grease we had to rub a bit of rough stone into the grease mark and the next time you scrubbed the floor it came off.

There was a wooden Methodist chapel in the village and they always had a service Sunday evening. The Anniversary was very important, held at the school, and on Whit Sunday they managed to get a piano on a farm wagon pulled by a horse and it would parade round the village with the little ones sat on the wagon, the girls all dressed in white. We also had some Quakers come once a year and one of the farmers would let them have some land to park this strange wooden caravan on; there were two ladies who used to run it. They came to the farm for eggs and milk in the hope that you would give it to them and they held little services in the caravan. I suppose they travelled around; they were nice people.

Ellen Spray

Rabbit Shooting

My father could track anything and catch a rabbit without even needing a gun. I've seen him look across towards Hillstown and say he could 'feel' rabbits in the field. I couldn't see anything but off he went with his walking stick and at a grass mound he'd take a swipe and a rabbit would roll out. In those days we were paying 1s 3d an hour for workers and that was top money. We could get half a crown a rabbit and I've seen us go out in the morning and get twenty rabbits. That was a lot of money in those days.

John Tinsley

Rabbit Pie

Dad would ask what we wanted for tea. If mother said rabbit, off he'd go down the fields, catch a rabbit and on the way back he'd gut it and skin it as he was walking along. By the time mum had it the rabbit was ready for cooking and beautifully fresh.

Jack Elliot

Tinsley Family

When I was a kid you could have raised an army of Tinsleys from round here, but when my generation dies out there will be about three. Most of the family still live around Spalding. I went down in 1962 and bought a gun. When I gave my name the gunsmith said, 'I'll put it on your account.' 'I haven't got an account,' says I. 'Oh you must have, all your family's got an account here. Spalding Home Grown Produce Company is run by Tinsleys.' So I could have had the gun for nothing!

John Tinsley

Two views of the Lancashire, Derbyshire and East Coast Line station at Carr Vale in 1951.

Home-Made Pork Pies

My grandfather was stationmaster at Bolsover. He came from Barton-on-Humber in Lincolnshire, where his family were farmers. My father told me how every year he would cycle there and grandfather's sister would load them up with pork pies as they killed their own pig. This was very useful as they had eight boys and one girl in the family. Grandmother's name was Prudence Nightingale.

Pam Ashley

Sutton Hall

I hate to see all the spaces in the village taken up. I miss those lovely crofts that we could walk in and enjoy the freedom of. I've been lucky because I've always lived on this front and you can watch the different changes of the field patterns. They are dark, then go golden and then dark again.

My grandmother lived at Sutton Scarsdale and when Sutton Hall was tumbling down grandfather knew a man that was in charge of getting rid of the doors. I remember going with mother and father once, and he took us round and showed us a hole in the floor where someone had fallen through. He gave us a piece of gilt picture framing from the hall. Unfortunately, on one occasion when five children were getting on her nerves, mother gave me a good whack with it and broke it. I cried my eyes out.

Ellen Spray

John Tinsley as a youngster in 1939.

Old Ted

Old Ted used to wear sacks round himself, tied round with binder twine. Edwin had said that he should live on the farm or he'd have to go to the Scarsdale workhouse. Edwin always shared his sweet ration with him.

Bessie Holmes

Village Hawkers

We had hawkers come into the village. One little man came with his straw basket, full with two-ounce squares of yeast. But he'd walk from wherever he came and when I think of

53

it, the yeast must have been beginning to work by the time he got here! Then we had another little man come with his barrel organ and mother used to say, 'Take this and give him a penny,' and then 'Oh, give him another,' and he'd play again, until mother's pennies had gone and he'd trundle away. We children thought it was marvellous.

Then we'd have the man who sharpened knives and the one who came selling pancheons, banging them together to show they weren't cracked. He'd chuck them up in the air and then he'd strike a bargain. One man came with an attaché case and it was full of buttons, cottons and safety pins. He'd come Monday morning when we were washing and mother would be pleased to stand for five minutes to get a break and have a look in his case. But where he came from and where he went I never knew. He measured the elastic on the lid of his case; that was his yard, whether it was or not. Then we'd have the greengrocer call, you could hear him calling from Hillstown. His horse was called Nobby and we could hear him call 'Nobby, whoa.' Then we had someone delivering paraffin and hardware, so you didn't really have to bother going out a lot and you didn't need to compare prices in the shops as it was all the same, wherever you went. Mother went out every ten days and she'd go to Chesterfield with just one pound.

Ellen Spray

Life on the Land

Occasionally we had a pig for the house; the others went as fat to Mansfield market. When I was ten we left Scarcliffe and came to Bole Appleton Farm. On the milk round I doled it out into half pint basins; it was 6d a pint. But when I got married I told mother I wouldn't do it any more; it would have to go on a lorry to the Milk Board. It was hard work. When father died at fifty-one, my mother went to Mr Botham at Chesterfield, the auctioneer, for his advice on what to do with the farm and he said, 'Well, Mrs Woods, you've got a good daughter here and a son and I would advise you to carry on.' When father died I had to do the milking. We had thirty-six cows and friends helped us with the harvest. We didn't have a holiday for years.

Bessie Holmes

Tuppenny Shepherd

One day old Joe Tinsley was working in the fields across Welbeck Road and he heard a shot. He could see Tuppenny Shepherd pick up a hare and hide it in the hedge bottom, show his dog where it was and then walk away. So, when Tuppenny had gone uncle Joe moved the hare about a hundred yards further up the hedge and showed his own dog where it was. Well, that night in the pub Tuppenny was bragging, 'I bet I've got the best dog in Bolsover. It'll fetch me a hare anytime I want one.' So, old Joe Tinsley started working him up and they finished up having a big bet for £5, which in the 1920s was a lot of money. So, Tuppenny sent the dog off, which came back with its tail between its legs and no hare. So Joe said 'Talk about the best dog, double or quits my dog can do better than that.' So, off it went and brought back the hare. Tuppenny looked at it. 'Why, this has been shot, its my hare!' But he didn't win the bet.

John Tinsley

Coalite Ground

The ground at Coalite which is now the stocking yard, we used to use for mushrooming and the land itself belonged to Mr Holmes at Mill Farm. We lived at Railway Cottages towards Markham Lane End and when farmer Holmes and his farm hands went to Bakewell show every year I was in charge of the horses at the farm. I used to ride them up Bolsover to the blacksmith's for shoeing and ride them back again. To a young boy that was really exciting.

Jack Elliot

Seed Time and Harvest

Miss Carter, an old friend of mine in the village – she died at ninety-two – used to say to me 'Oh, I do miss the rollers.' That was in the spring when the farmer was busy sowing seed and rolling the land. The disc rollers made a din on the road even with a horse pulling them and it reminded her of spring. I remember we had some big farm horses and dad when he came into

The Cousins family photographed outside the castle in the 1880s. The eldest, Fanny, stands at the back and in the middle, from left to right, are Sally, Julia and Ada. The two boys, Lewis and John, are in front. Lewis, the youngest, is wearing a 'hand-me-down' dress from his sister, a common occurrence in poor families of this time.

the yard used to lift me up and I'd cling to the horses' reins. He'd let me sit on till she walked into the stable. I used to help a bit when I was quite small.

To make a haystack then, they used to have a picker pole – a long pole with a grabber on a rope coming down from it – and the rope was attached to a horse and hay was raised on to the stack. I helped with that by leading the horse and with the potato picking and singling turnips and chopping mangles. This was quite an art because you had to

A label of the Bolsover Jam Company, which survived in the town until the early 1950s.

leave a row of leaves tidy and it was the way you chopped each row. We always helped stooking corn, father showed us how to bend our knees and waft it in. That's how we learnt how to do it. We all had to help because we didn't employ a lot of labour. We had a lad of about fourteen, then my brother went on the farm when he was sixteen. He went to the grammar school but came straight back and really took over from dad. We also kept sheep and dad was more a shepherd than anything else.

Ellen Spray

CHAPTER 4

Childhood and Schooldays

Bolsover Guides and Brownies examine the goodies in their sales stall in the 1960s.

The German Scout visit to Bolsover in July 1970. Bottom right is Lilian Phipps, District Guide Commissioner. In the centre are Cllr Sid Fisher and Mrs Fisher. Behind them is Fred Rollin, town clerk, with Mrs Rollin. Jack Elliott is the third Scout from the left at the back.

Water Play

There is a little stream in the valley, it's from the river Poulter originally, and we'd play in it with straw boats and eat what we called pig nuts, digging for them with a pen knife. They were like little hard potatoes and you rubbed them on your clothes before eating them. Then there was an almond-shaped leaf which we chewed; it was a bit minty. There was also 'bread and cheese' which was young hawthorn bud which we picked and ate. We always knew what to look for.

Ellen Spray

Starting School

I went to Chesterfield School and people though it a bit of a soft touch if you went there, but in fact it was the hardest school about. Do anything wrong and you had to write out Matthew Chapter One, and that's a killer! You had to fight for a seat on the bus. My first morning I was outside Jack Eyre's at ten minutes past seven. The bus went at a quarter past eight but I wanted to be the first in the queue. Well, the bus came and there was a mad rush. I'd never seen anything like it, but

Johnson, his father was a tiler on Middle Street, gave me two hundred lines, 'I must not fight to get on the bus' and the following week it was Matthew Chapter One. Well. I thought this was a bit rough, 'if I'm going to get lines I'm going to earn them.' So after that I really fought to get on that bus!

John Tinsley

School Cane

School in the Model Village was a bit tough. Cane was a regular thing. One teacher was called Arthur Miller, big chap with a bit of meat on him. He looked a bit of a brute. On one occasion we'd just had an arithmetic test and he said that for every sum that was wrong we'd get one stroke of the cane and on mine there were five sums wrong, so I bent over five times. The same day, because I wasn't quiet, this other teacher, Pa Hollis we used to call him – he lived in the cottages at Markham Cross Roads – 'Bentley,' he said, 'Out.' I had to go to t'front and get another one. Today, they don't know they're born in school.

Alf Bentley

Tea at the Castle

I remember going to tea with Mrs Radford who lived at the castle and the cat was on the table licking the butter. 'Oh well, he likes it,' said Mrs Radford to mother. Jack Radford used to run along the battlements cursing local children. He was a really frightening

Mrs Jack Radford as a young teacher.

character, small dark and deformed, a most uncivilized man. They lived in the amazingly cold rooms above the Castle Riding School.

Pam Ashley

Starting Out

When I finished at the High School it was the beginning of the Great War and a friend of mine was the headmistress of Palterton school and she wanted a teacher. So, she said, 'Well, you've been to the High School, you can do it.' So I went even though I couldn't teach and didn't want to. I'd been studying shorthand and typing.

59

Plodding home along Welbeck Road, before the Second World War. Marl House stands to the left.

Anyway, the HMI came out and fortunately for me I thought she was the school nurse and, as I didn't know who she was, gave an extremely good lesson! I used to cycle from school to the vicarage at Scarcliffe as the vicar was the person who paid us.

From Palterton I went to teach at Arkwright Town and that was very different; a different class of people. However, I'd always wanted to be a receptionist so I went off to Swanage to train. Then I went to Jersey and became a chauffeur, driving the Island Judge to Parliament.

Kath Palmer

School

I have a great sentimental feeling for the Church School; it was second to none. We were taken to church regularly and the Curate used to come twice a week for scripture lessons. We were entered for scripture examinations. I remember the school catching fire and the new brick part opening during the 1893 coal strike.

Ethel Hodkin (recorded 1973)

School Train

You could catch the train at Scarcliffe and get off in Skegness, something you certainly couldn't do today. It cost a shilling return and if the church choir went we all paid a further shilling for the tea.

Everyone travelled by train in those days. I went to school in Shirebrook by train and it was only two miles away. The stationmaster always greeted each train decked out in a top hat. He was so proud of the station and it often won a prize for the best kept station on the line.

Norah Ley

Playing Hooky

At Scarcliffe School we had allotment gardens and the lads did the gardening. My brother had a friend, Bogo Chapel, who lived at Palterton and they used to be gone. No one ever missed them and they'd go bird's nesting, right through the woods to

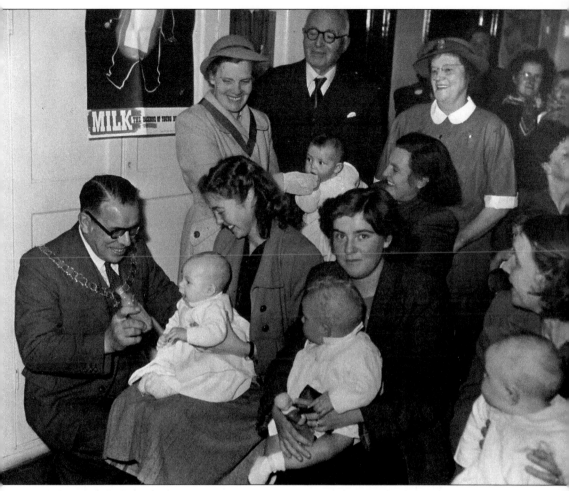

Welbeck Road Clinic in 1953. Councillor Sid Fisher and Mrs Fisher join Dr A.H. Wear, Medical Officer of Health for Bolsover UDC, and Nurse Blood giving babies their free orange juice.

Langwith. My brother had over two hundred birds' eggs, but there were never enough children at school for them not to be missed, so whether or not the teacher wanted them out of the way or not I don't know. And it's funny, you know: my mother never knew he'd played hooky, and I never said a word.

Bessie Holmes

Carless

Young people could roam at will before the war. We used to roller-skate down the middle of Welbeck Road, across the main Rotherham Road to the quarry at Whaley. There was so little traffic.

Pam Ashley

Teaching Trials

At Welbeck Road School there were 250 boys. Well, every boy knew every teacher and every teacher knew every boy and you got this wonderful trust and confidence, and it lasts. Jim Brown, Tom Wragg, Dennis Riley – we still have the same good relationship. As a pupil teacher you had to construct your own lesson and I can remember trying to find something to fill a lesson. It was almost impossible at sixteen having to talk for fifty minutes.

I got a job at Killamarsh as an uncertificated teacher, for four years. I got less than the caretaker and we all had to take a ten per cent cut in wages as the government was in a mess. I went to York Teacher Training College. It was a Church of England College and you were allowed out two nights a week and had to be in by 9.30 p.m. Discipline was like being in junior school today. You had lectures in the morning, sport in the afternoon, you had lectures again until seven o'clock and then into your study for work. There was no latitude at all.

Ken Leaning

An Extra Finger

My brother had a second finger on one joint and when he was born the doctor said to let him get older before they'd remove it. Then, when he was four, my mother wanted it done before he went to school and the doctor said, 'No, I shall leave it; he's got used to it now.'

Bessie Holmes

School Clinic

I remember the school clinic and on one occasion I had to see the dentist and have a tooth extracted. In this room was an enormous chair and an enormous nurse to go with it. The tooth was very reluctant to come out so the nurse ended up kneeling on my stomach and withdrawing it by force.

David Joyce

I absolutely dreaded the school dental service and being taken to the Chesterfield Clinic below the police court. I had many fillings and was often sick on the doorstep before I went in! On the day I had my tonsils out I had to go to the same clinic by bus. On the way back, again by bus, I felt so poorly, and had ice cream as a treat. I still cannot drink Bovril, it is so reminiscent of mouth wash.

Betty Hunter

TB

A lot of my friends died young; TB was a killer. There were TB hospitals at Langwith and Mastin Moor.

Ethel Hodkin

Decontamination

Our school was a decontamination centre. I remember the men coming back from Dunkirk and sitting in the playground absolutely exhausted and a high pile of khaki clothes, smelling to high heaven. I suppose they'd been soaked in the sea.

Joyce Leaning

School Life

Father came to be headmaster of Shuttlewood School in 1908. That was a blacklist school and he was given a free hand to do whatever he liked to bring it up to standard. In those days schools were rough places and it was a mining area. I remember him telling me that in his first week one of the thirteen-year-olds threw a slate at him but eventually when the boy grew up he became one of my father's canvassers at the election and a great friend.

In 1912 he came up to Welbeck Road as head – it was a new mixed school for seven to fourteen-year-olds. It was formal, very well organized, I don't remember the slightest bit of bullying in those days. His desk was in the hall and his cane was always on the desk as a warning! He used to take singing for the whole school, all the old songs and one of the things I vividly remember every Armistice Day was that the whole school walked to the Cenotaph for the service. That was quite moving.

When I was nine I took the scholarship. There were very few in those days and we had to go down to New Bolsover school then, which is now demolished, and sit in the hall, a huge hall. It was very terrifying at nine and two of us got the scholarship to Chesterfield High School. So from ten to seventeen I went there.

When we started the day the whole school was in the hall for assembly. We

Mr H.W. Day (Gaffer Day), head of Shuttlewood and later Welbeck Road School. He later became a councillor, providing many years of service to the town.

also had clean boot inspection; woe betide you if you had dirty boots or shoes. Everybody had to have a handkerchief and show it, or a bit of a rag.

My father lived in Bolsover of course and everybody knew Gaffer Day and if anyone did anything wrong he was there. The parents always backed him up and they respected the teachers.

Joyce Leaning

The view from Station Road into the Market Place in the 1950s.

Fifty in a Class

When I returned to Bolsover from teaching in London in the 1950s we sat at a high wooden teacher's desk and found the classroom was absolutely full with fifty children. You couldn't get any displays or anything else in. I'd come from college with all these big ideas and it was hard to implement anything but basic teaching. There was no room for all the children if they didn't all do the same thing at once.

Pam Ashley

Rivals

Bottom Bolsover and Top Bolsover were two different communities. As a kid, up Hill Top we were Welbeck Roaders (The School) and the 'Nats' (National School) and New Bolsover was separate. There was rivalry between the three schools.

Joyce Leaning

School Lift

From Railway Cottages it was a long walk to school up the hill. So if I was late I'd listen for a car on the road. This, remember, was the 1930s when there were few cars in Bolsover, just the odd bus. At seven minutes to nine I'd hear it; the headmaster's car at Markham Lane Ends. I'd doff my hat as it approached, he'd slow down and say jump in; I can't see that happening now.

Jack Elliot

Cundy House

The Cundy House had inside a rising spring of cool, clear water. My sister, when she came home from school, would walk across the Parks and up by the Cundy House and she always used to take a bottle so she could have a drink from the water.

Kath Palmer

High Flyer

Dr Gordon's brother was a pilot and on one occasion he actually flew around Bolsover, circling the house on Oxcroft Lane. As children we all stood on the little balcony waving to him. We could see his face clearly in the cockpit.

Anne Joyce

Early Start

You've heard the joke about the boy who ran away from school to join the circus, well I ran away from home to go to school. At four and a half I went down Station Road and presented myself at New Bolsover School. It was the day they were having their photos taken. I had mine taken and then the headmaster's daughter took me home. I still have the photo.

Jack Elliot

First Buses

Transport of course wasn't so good in those days so you tended to stay here. I can remember the first buses labouring up Bolsover Hill when I was a child, tiny buses they were. I remember having to go on the bus to Chesterfield to have my tonsils out at the clinic and I came back on the bus on the same day! Terrifying it was. A neighbour took me and I felt absolutely wicked.

Joyce Leaning

Christmas Boots

Every Christmas I would have bought for me a new pair of boots from Hilton's shoe shop in the Market Place. Father Christmas always arrived in the shop, in person, to deliver them!

Ada Riley

The Choice

When I was sixteen I went as a pupil teacher to Welbeck Road School and I would be sitting in or trying to teach children two years younger than me. In Bolsover there were only two things to do; go down Bolsover Colliery or teach.

Ken Leaning

Teas and Maids

I remember Mrs Sykes at Sherwood Lodge because she was a friend of my Aunt Emmy Stevenson. I was regularly taken to walk in the gardens and to play croquet. Mrs Sykes had hoops on the lawn and she would have the mallets brought out. Mrs Sykes and my aunt, both dressed in black, would sit on the lawn while a maid would bring tea out.

Pam Ashley

Pancake Day

At the Colliery School it was Mr Haddock the headmaster and he was very fair and his wife was also but some of the others were a bit too strict. We always used to have a half-day holiday at Shrove Tuesday with girls with battledore and lads with whip and top. At home mum would have a stack of pancakes ready.

A.W.

Teaching

I taught at New Bolsover School but I wasn't too keen on the headmistress, Miss Varney. It was my first placement and she would stand behind me, peeping over my shoulder and correcting me. We had classes of forty in those days, mind you they sat in rows, they weren't dotted around four to a table. I didn't like it so I moved to Ashbourne. I qualified through a correspondence course by taking the course at the High School, St Helena's. I was at New Bolsover for just two years and this post was advertised at Ashbourne and I said to mother. 'I think I'll take it, I'm not obliged to stay if I don't like it.' I stayed from 1925 to 1950! When the post at Palterton was advertised, my sister who was teaching there said, 'Why don't you apply and come home?' I think she wanted the company as well, so I did and was quite happy there, teaching until 1963 when I retired. It was easier teaching at Palterton than New Bolsover. We had only one boy who was any trouble at all and Miss Street, the headmistress, was taking a geography lesson and they had to take notes. He said, 'I can't find my pencil, Miss,' so Miss Street said, 'Right, while you're finding your pencil I'll find my cane.' There was a cane in a glass cupboard and he said, 'I've found my pencil, Miss.' 'Yes,' said Miss Street, 'and I've found my cane.' There was no trouble after that but when he left school he went to work in the farm at the Grange on Scarcliffe Lane and he'd only been working there about six months when we next heard he was in prison. He was the only boy in the whole school who was any trouble at all.

It was easier teaching children at Palterton. They were mainly farmers' children. At New Bolsover they were a bit rough and ready.

Ada Bagshaw

Prison Visiting

The police station was at the top of Hockley and it had a little prison with one cell. As children we would walk down Hockley and peep through the window to see if we could see the prisoner in his cell.

Kath Palmer

The Gas Man Cometh

I remember the gas street lamps and Mr Middleton coming along every night to trim the wicks, alter the lamp and turn the gas on. He had to carry the ladder around with him and maintain every lamp individually. It's like another world.

Pam Ashley

Childhood in the 1920s

As a child in the 1920s I read comics like Rainbow. I was fascinated with elephants who dressed and talked. Rin Tin Tin, the cowboy's dog, also featured. I also remember some missionary stories.

Mother bought toys for us at Piper's Penny Bazaar in Chesterfield: whips and tops, skipping ropes, shuttlecock, dominoes, tiddlywinks, that sort of

Teachers all: Kit Bagshaw, Connie Street (headmistress of Palterton School), and Ada Bagshaw, photographed at Blackpool in the 1960s.

thing. Toys in those days were seasonal. I also had a china doll in a pram. In those days, you could play in the castle grounds and the 'dungeons', chased off by Jack Radford. We played on the Hornscroft and made dens in the entrenchment. I always had to be 'degrimed' on the seat of my knickers from where we slid down the slopes on our bums. We took picnics there consisting of jam sandwiches and bottles of water. At bluebell time we were taken round the Ramper and picked flowers in the little copse at the end of Oxcroft.

Betty Hunter

Vic Feather, president of the TUC, presents the prizes at Bolsover School in the 1960s. Second from the left is Bruce Canning (headmaster), and in the centre is Cllr Joyce Platts (chair of the County Education Committee). On the right is Cllr Sid Fisher.

Frustrated Hens

At Welbeck Road Boys' School in the 1950s there were former air-raid shelters which from the outside looked just like grass mounds. Inside we kept poultry and all the eggs and vegetables we grew in the school grounds were used for school dinners. I was in charge of poultry and the lads would sit watching the eggs pop out of the hens. When we saw an egg coming out we'd try and push it back in again. They were not happy hens!

David Joyce

The Corner Shop

When I married Albert in 1944 and came here to Dane Bank, that part of the shop nearest the Bull was the front sitting room and Albert's mother told me that there was always a suit of armour in the window.

In the 1940s there was only one other shop sold fruit and veg, and we had the wartime allocation of certain fruits such as bananas which were delivered by Ernest Shentall's at Chesterfield. Being wartime everything was rationed and people would queue up outside when they saw Shentall's lorry pull up. It was a big occasion during the war when rationed food was delivered. We used to deliver in this old van to Duckmanton, Scarcliffe, Palterton, all the villages round.

Bolsover was a mass of little grocery shops in those days. There was Wakefield's over the road, Mary Blatherwick up Welbeck Road, Winifred Yates, Daisy Lynn. I think there's only me left now. The supermarkets have killed them all off. In those days people didn't have cars or refrigerators so local shops were most important. Every day folk from Cow Tail Row came in for 'threepenn' orth of pot herbs'. They wanted a carrot, a parsnip, an onion and a small turnip. It was so regular, they had it day in day out. You knew what they wanted before they came in.

When the post office and the dole office moved from this side of town we were affected, as people do not want to walk far. Yellow lines were another killer. Before them all the lorries going down to Coalite and the pit would stop outside, but yellow lines stopped that. All these things took a bit more business away from us.

Scarratt's shop down Hockley was amazing. You could buy anything at Scarratt's, pots and pans, wallpaper, paint, hardware. When we did the shop on a Monday, grandma used to say, 'Run down to Scarratt's for a penny roll of wallpaper, Anne,' and we'd dress the window.

Anne Woodhouse

The Dentist

By common consent Mr Rossell was clean but not too good a dentist and Mr Kennington was dirty and a very good dentist!

Anne Joyce

Personal Service

Woodhead's shop in the Market Place had a cash system where a lady sat at the cash till and put the money into a small circular hollow disc. It 'pinged' and shot off around the shop on a pulley system. As a child I was absolutely fascinated with this. Everything was sold loose from a large mahogany counter and weighed out in blue bags. The smell of the shop was quite amazing, home cured bacon which was sliced from the bone, dried fruits and butter. The first job my mother had was travelling around on a bike taking orders for Woodhead's. This was followed by boys on delivery bikes taking complete orders round to the farms and outlying areas. Very few people then had phones so orders had to be collected in person. Everything was personal service in those days.

Pam Ashley

Coalite

I first became aware of the smell from coalite during the war. The local explanation was they were making mustard gas, for the war effort!

In 1960 when I first visited a consultant about my arthritis he asked me where I lived as a child. When I replied Railway Cottages, opposite Coalite, he asked where we got our milk

Cllr Jack Spray receives a presentation from Cllr Stan Clarke. Also pictured are: Jack Walton, Joe Mason, Fred Rollin, Sid Fisher, Charles Margerrison and Daisy Marples.

from. When I said Mill Farm he then asked if it was pasteurized. It wasn't of course, it was straight from the cow and water-cooled. 'Well, that figures,' said the consultant. He said no more.

Jack Elliot

Bolsover Doctors

D r Stratton fell down in an air-raid shelter in his Langwith Road garden. He broke his neck. Dr Saville was the gentleman's doctor and used to ride around on a high-stepping horse. His daughters had a donkey cart and my father's elder brother was walking along the Ramper one day when he saw Dr

Saville's daughters in their cart and thrashing out at the donkey which refused to move. So, uncle picked a handful of dead grass, lifted up its tail and lit a match to it and away it went! The last time he saw it they were racing towards Elmton Park with Dr Saville's daughters hanging onto the reins like grim death, followed by a steam of smoke.

John Tinsley

Ratting

S ome of the happiest days of my life were spent ratting with Todge Torr, the Bolsover rabbit catcher; a real Carr

Vale character he was. He was an orphan brought up at Bainbridge Hall orphanage and a mate of my dad's.

He'd sit in our doorway waiting for dad, dressed in a colourful muffler and a big trilby hat. He had one of the best dogs in the world. Still and obedient, that dog was a real professional rat catcher. Todge would study the farm building where the rats were, examine the entry holes, put his ferret in and wait with his dog for them to come out. It was quite scientific really. If his dog wasn't sure Todge would say he wanted a second opinion and he'd get down to the hole and have a sniff himself. He always knew if they were there or not. He'd place a tin lid over the holes and if it moved he'd know the rats were there.

Later, during the war the rat catcher was paid by the council, so much for each rat caught. You had to prove the number by taking them to the council. Well, at Mill Farm we had a haystack that was alive with rats and we called Todge in. He caught hundreds, put them on his cart and wheeled them up Bolsover to the council offices. When they asked where he'd caught them and he replied 'Mill Farm' they said they didn't want them as the farm was over the council boundary, in Chesterfield Rural District. So he was left with a barrow full of dead rats!

Jack Elliot

Castle Coaches

We started Castle Coaches in 1954 and ran it for thirty years. In the early days there was no other bus company in Bolsover, except Flints at

Welbeck Road swimming team. Clockwise from the top left: Marjorie Webster, Stella Smith, Iris Bird and Mary Cooper.

Carr Vale, a little bus that used to run up and down the hill, and pit buses to Glapwell Colliery.

One day my husband Albert came home from the pit and said he'd never go down again. And he didn't. I never knew what prompted this but he decided to get out while he was still fit and not injured in any way. He'd been down since the age of thirteen. Albert was always mad on driving and had an Austin Atlantic. Well, one evening he saw an advert in the *Star*. Alan Whetton at Brimington, who was a coach proprietor, wanted an Austin Atlantic. We went to see him and by midnight we'd decided he could have

Castle Coaches in the Market Place, in the late 1950s.

the car in exchange for one of his twenty-nine-seater coaches. And that's how we started. We had to demolish the boundary wall in order to get it into the yard. Eventually we built up a fleet and by the time Albert died we had thirteen coaches. They were all parked like dominoes in the yard.

We did school and swimming bath runs, WI and Mothers' Union outings, that sort of thing. Albert lined them up in the Market Place. After a couple of years we bought a brand new fifty-two-seater couch from the makers in Scarborough and at that time we'd just had my daughter Jane, so we called it *Lady Jane*. They all had a name after that. Albert really did love coaching. The thing was you saw everything; flower shows, race meetings, theatre shows, and of course you went abroad. We had working men's clubs outings,

cricket clubs, brass and silver band concerts, they all used us.

In those days there were no restrictions on how many hours you could drive without a rest. He'd come in at midnight and I'd be waiting with a dustpan and brush to clean out and Albert would be gone again at seven in the morning. We hadn't got a fuel tank at that time and old Jack Eyre would keep his pumps open until Albert got back late at night. He'd come across the Market Place, tap on the window and say, 'Is he back yet? Tell him not to fill up anywhere else!'

Anne Woodhouse

Mrs Ray Howarth steps aboard *My Lady*.

Undertaking

The very first job I had was with Merill Stubbins, the undertaker. I got 6d an hour sweeping the joiner's shop, but only if it didn't rain.

Alf Bentley

Just Desserts

My grandfather was a Wylde. They came from a cottage near Southgate Crossroads and moved to Bolsover, to a shop which is now The Wellspring. They were saddlers and leather workers. My grandmother married William Hunt and they lived in Middle Street until 1904 when they moved to the Town End farm on what is now Moor Lane. Grandfather died young, but my grandmother lived to be ninety-nine and her sister a hundred and one.

Fred Hunt, my uncle, was a likely sort of chap, but I only remember him getting done once by the police and that was through a chap called Luther Fern. He was a special constable and one night someone opened the gate to one of Fred's fields, letting one of his beasts out. Anyway, Luther Fern had him fined two pounds for having a beast on the road. A little while later Fred was coming back from Chesterfield, up Cemetery Hill at Hady when he passed two people in evening dress. He stopped to give them a lift and who should it be but Luther Fern and his landlady. So Fred pulled down his window and said, 'Good evening, Mr Fern,' and drove on.

Grandmother Hunt of Hunt's farm, Moor Lane, as a young woman and fifty years later outside the farm.

When Fern saw him later he said, 'That was a nasty thing to do, Fred Hunt.' 'Yes,' said Fred, 'and it was a nasty thing to report my beast to the constable. I think we're level now.'

John Tinsley

Welbeck Road Flourmill

We had a windmill with sails with twenty steps going up to it, although I never remember the sails going round. We were never allowed to go inside because the floors were rotting. Opposite the windmill was the old mill where they used to grind corn and I remember my father and uncle wearing masks over their mouths and seeing bags of corn coming down from the top to the bottom. There was an engine room which drove the machinery, I remember that. There was a very tall chimney which had to be demolished and various stables leading off. That would be around 1910.

Ada Bagshaw

In Service

We had a maid, although she didn't live in. She used to live on Hill Top and come early morning across the Parks, up the back lane every day. She was a grand girl; Gladys Gascoigne she was. She stayed all day and went home in the evening and then when I had the babies she helped look after them as well. We also had a gardener who was a little old man with a long white beard. He was an odd-job man at the brick works. There was a garden at the side of that and he used to come up and do mother's garden also.

Dorothy Cutts

Railway Romance

Mrs Rowlett kept a shop at Lea Home Estate, in the bungalow at the top. Her husband was signalman at Markham Junction. There were only five trains a day but he was an important man. Their daughter was a pedal-biking spinster who was clerk at the LNER station; bun, spectacles, big hat, the lot. She eventually married the man who built the Doe Lea Bridge, Tommy Drabble. Every day Miss Rowlett had to push her bike across the new bridge to the station. They met and married.

Jack Elliot

Council Functions

When we first came the council always held a function at Christmas. It was the Christmas Dinner, held in the colliery schools and it was black tie, dinner jackets, with the ladies in long dresses and gloves: a proper function. The coal board had presented the Chairman's chain and a coalite brooch for his lady.

The Coal Board would always help in an emergency. When the church fire occurred in 1960, Charles rang them and they said, 'Just let us know what you want.' At the building of the bandstand in Sherwood Lodge Coalite had a crane, and when Charles wanted it, they simply asked when. He replied 'now' and it was there within the hour. When the council wanted to build they always contacted the coal board for advice as to how the land lay and where they would be mining next. That's why not a lot of new developments were built at the top of the hill. There was always trouble with the Moor Lane Estate sewers. As it was so flat there was no fall and they needed a pump, which tended to fill and split.

Bunty Margerrison

Young Worker

My eldest sister went into service when she was eleven.

William Spray

Allowance Rations

My grandfather came from Killamarsh to work at the pit. He originally lived in a cottage at Pit Fields, near the entrance to what is now Darwood Lane. He was a buttyman and they soon moved to New Bolsover and eventually to Church Street. Here they rented a shop but it was very much hand to mouth in the early days. They would buy goods from the market, going off with Charlie the pony and trap,

Bolsover UDC dinner in 1961. Harold Neal, MP for Bolsover, is first left, Cllr Sid Fisher is in the centre, the Revd W. Speakman in standing to the right of centre and Mrs Speakman is seated to the far right.

return home, sell them and then close the shop until they brought more goods to sell.

These 'Allowance Rations' during the First World War meant that you could only buy so much until the next allowance. They bought sweets and confectionery from the Sherwood Confectionery in Worksop and went to T.H. Collins in Mansfield for sweets and tobacco.

Anne Joyce

Bolsover Mortuary

I lived round t'corner on Church Street, where t'library is now and Doctor McKay used to call me round to t'mortuary when he was cutting folks up. When he sawed their heads off he'd place one of those metal hooks round their heads; Mrs Margerrison's son has them now and he'd saw away and he'd sew them up with binder twine. There was only room for one body on t'table so he'd have two or three others stacked up around, waiting.

Joe Mason

Workhouse

The Workhouse was Scarsdale in Chesterfield. Once in you never got out. If you lost your mind you went to

Civic Dinner. Included here are Dorothy Woodhouse, Eddie Collier, Sheila and Noel Bagguley, Jack and Christine Walton, Anne and Albert Woodhouse, and Elsie and Fred Rollin.

Mickleover [County Mental Asylum]. There was only parish pay then, no old age pension. You had to apply to the Board of Guardians for relief and it was paid out in the Tythe Barn.

If you had children and they didn't go to school money wasn't paid. Those people were called paupers.

Ethel Hodkin (recorded 1972)

Lady Georgiana

I remember the Town Clerk telling my husband, who was the Chief Surveyor to the council, about a church near Tuxford in Lincolnshire, built by the Duke of Newcastle. They had a small Saxon church at East Markham and the Duke wanted a bigger one and he built a beauty, about 1830. All the villagers were instructed to go there and they hated it. When the Duke died they all returned to worship at the Saxon building. We went along to look at both churches and in the new one it was like the Marie Celeste; there were things on the altar, hymn books lying on the pews, just like they'd all gone into the next room, intending to return. Well, Charles was very taken with a marble statue of the Duchess of Newcastle. Beautiful it was, in Westmacott marble but it was getting vandalized and this upset him. So, he got hold of Noel Bagguley, Geoff Hawkes and Ken Davison and they went along to board the place up. When local people asked what on earth they were doing he told them he was saving their church! They removed the memorial to Clumber chapel. Revd Speakman was very good at attending to the ecclesiastical side of things and a monumental mason from Lincoln cathedral came over to supervise its move. Well, within twelve months East Markham came to the notice of the distressed churches organization and they wanted to know where the memorial had vanished to. So, it went back. Charles would do things like that. He was so enthusiastic. If he took anything on that was it. But it was incredible the number of Bolsover people involved in this removal of a memorial from a strange church.

Bunty Margerrison

Variety

The Woodhouse family has changed business with the times. Roland Woodhouse had a pet shop on Town End and followed this with a bookies. I extended from general store to pet shop supplies. Loreen Woodhouse ran a toy shop and subscription library in the Market Place then went into babywear. We've all done a bit of all sorts.

Anne Woodhouse

Pits and Pubs

We lived on Hill Top and I remember the coal strike in 1893. I was taken by my parents to the top of the Crags to watch the soldiers come from Sheffield and the shopkeepers had to board up their shops. The men were out about nineteen weeks.

My father worked at Glapwell Colliery and he travelled by the mail run which started at Dronfield. It cost him sixpence a week to travel from Bolsover to Glapwell. The train was just wooden seats and ran at 6 a.m. from the old Midland station. When the miners were on afternoons and nights they had to walk there and back. My father was a Lincolnshire man who came to Bolsover when he was ten years old. My mother was born a Revill at the Old Thatch public house on Hill Top in1861. Grandma kept the pub and I remember her making oat cakes and pykelets and knitting stockings for the people at the castle.

The pub was the only one between here and the Travellers' Rest at Shuttlewood. Great Grandma who had been a Whittaker was born in 1800. The Old Thatch was a free house and the beer came from a Sheffield brewery. I was brought up on beer! Great grandfather John Whittaker was a one-armed man who drove a carrier's cart to Chesterfield twice a week. My father came from a farming family in Lincolnshire, at a time when life on the land was very difficult. The Staveley Coal and Iron Company were sinking pits at Hartington, Seymour and the two Markhams, so he came.

My grandfather, Reuben Revill, was born on the Sutton Estate. He later kept the Anchor public house but started life in Seymour pit when he was eleven years old and walked from Bolsover each day across Woodhouse Lane to Seymour. He never had a day's schooling in his life but became manager at Markham Pit. When he developed a serious illness he moved to run the Anchor. It was a meeting place for old Parson Hills and the local doctors. My parents were very keen on politics, they were Conservatives.

Ethel Hodkin (on the right), whose memories stretch back to the 1890s.

I told Margerrison [Charles Margerrison, former surveyor to Bolsover Urban District Council] 'Ay up, shut up. I was brought up on Brampton beer and Conservative politics!' That floored him. I can see the old tap room now, all those old men with Dr Spencer and Parson Hills sitting round on hard wooden benches and discussing politics with my parents. There were two tap rooms and a parlour. Beer was $\frac{1}{2}$d in the Parlour. Best beer was 3d a pint. Whisky 3s 6d a bottle, gin 2s 10d. Bitter beer was not drawn from the pumps, it was fetched in a jug from the barrels in the cellar. Father used to say it had restorative powers and people used it as a tonic. Most of the publics were Chesterfield Brewery, but the Anchor was Brampton.

I remember the Cross Keys being built. It was a little old tumble down public and you went down steps from the Market Place. A man named Carter kept it for years. The Swan is the oldest public, with a stone parlour where the Duke of Portland held his court. It was open six o'clock in the morning till eleven o'clock at night. He did close Sunday afternoons. As there were no children's licensing acts in those days the children drank beer at dinnertime and at night.

We used to play around the cross in the old Market Place. It was four square with steps. I remember election results being read from there. The new Market Place was called the Market Square.

I went to the Church School, but my mother attended a small private school run by Mrs Booker in Castle Street. Later she paid 3d a week to go to the Church School. My first school was at the top of Cotton Street in the old tithe barn.

Ethel Hodkin (recorded 1973)

William Barfoot in Castle Street with one of his lorries.

Barfoot Businesses

Eventually Barfoot's moved to Castle Street where they farmed, ran a huge haulage business which carried coal and also bricks from the brickyard. They also had a restaurant and a shop which sold ice cream by the glass with dairy cream poured on it. Their sherry trifle was famous in Bolsover and we make it still in the family. The Barfoot milk float was pulled by Tommy the horse. He was a handful and often ran away with the milk so the wheel had to be fastened to restrain him.

Anne Joyce

Transport

The first doctor in Bolsover to own a car was Dr Spencer. Jack Bagshaw at the mill had one with a tiller, not a steering wheel. The first form of heavy transport I remember seeing in Bolsover was a steam lorry which brought beer from Mansfield and Nottingham. There was a carrier cart service and Twidle's wagonette took the mails to Chesterfield by horse and trap. Underwood's buses started in 1919. They were former war vehicles. The corporation buses couldn't get up the hill from Chesterfield so they stopped at the bottom. Twidle's ran between Hillstown, Palterton and Scarcliffe.

William Spray (recorded 1972)

Early Electronics

My father Bert Leaning wanted to go to the grammar school but there was no money to send him. So, as he was always keen on electrics, he became an electrician at the pit. Then he decided to open his own business. There was a little wooden shed at the side of the garden by my aunt's cottage in Town End and he started in there. He started making crystal wireless sets. They worked on accumulator batteries and he would charge them up for people who brought them to the shop. At home, on Welbeck Road we had what we called a 'charging shed'. He was always keen on electrics. Today he would have been very happy in the modern electronics industry. Everyone knew him, he was in such a prominent position in Town End and his business developed from those early radios to domestic appliances between the wars. I remember the Hoover we had which I'd inherited from my mother on getting married. When I was teaching, the Hoover rep called at school to service it. He was on his hands and knees when I decided to get rid of it asking for first refusal and eventually it went to a museum.

Although dad sold early washers and home appliances money was very short in the 1930s and '40s and many people paid weekly. Both Dennis Riley and Frank Smith worked for him as apprentices, eventually opening their own business. Frank bought dad's business from him on retirement.

We had a telephone, which was quite unusual in Bolsover shortly after the war, and when television arrived we had to have it taken out because people would ring at all times of the day or night and ask dad to go and repair their TV and, of course, in the early days they were always going wrong.

Pam Ashley

Co-Operation

All the families round about had their own Co-op. My father being on the railway didn't get concessionary coal but the miners had more than they knew what to do with. So, we'd be given coal in exchange for wood from our store. Often families would barter eggs from their fowls for home grown vegetables. They were lovely people, all honest working men. There was never any nastiness.

Jack Elliot

Bert Leaning and his family in their Bullnose Morris, 1929.

Market Place Shops

I remember Woodhead's shop at the top of the Market Place, at the bottom was Hilton's Shoe Shop and Eyres at the top. Jack Eyre had petrol pumps. On the other side was Meadow Dairy, Rayner the watchmaker and on the corner Wycherley's. There was always the Beehive on Town End and then the little grocery shop, Watkinson's, at the corner of the yard in Town End. On the other side was the old picture house and Mr Pitkin's garage.

Ada Bagshaw

Bolsover Market Place at the turn of the century. The centre archway now leads into the Cotton Street Market from Middle Street.

Urban District Council

My father was on the council for over thirty years and what amazes us now is that you've got these huge council offices and in those days six people ran Bolsover!

My father went on the council in 1913 because my brother got diphtheria through earth closets. There was an epidemic and father was so furious he decided to do something about it. He was a member of all the committees including Chesterfield and Bolsover Water Board. When the water tower at Hillstown opened he was given a gold key and had to go to Parliament to see the bill through. He worked very hard for Bolsover. It's in the blood of our family; my brother in Lincolnshire was County Councillor and Mayor of his town and my brother in Chesterfield was Mayor and given freedom of the Borough. I was brought up to believe that service to others was the most important thing and not to think of yourself.

My father was Independent and would never attach any label to himself. He didn't believe in local politics. The others were nearly all Labour but he always topped the polls. In those days people went to councillors with their problems, they didn't go to an office, and he spent council money as though it was his own.

Joyce Leaning

Bandstand

I built the bandstand in Sherwood Lodge. It was built for the twinning ceremony with Decazeville and Charles

Sherwood Lodge and bandstand in the 1960s.

Margerrison designed it. There were two pillars, one at each end and t'council were building with Wimpey's at the time, down on Bainbridge Road and Charles and the Wimpey man would watch me from his office across t'lawn. They'd come wandering across and when these pillars were about a foot high they'd say 'I think you'd better move them back a bit,' so I'd do it. And this kept happening. I think I built the same pillar four times!

Joe Mason

Cotton Street

There used to be four houses opposite where the library is now. My grandma lived in the end one all her life and outside there were big pavers and I was only saying to someone last week that from being eighteen to getting married I use to

have to scrub those every week. She said, 'Well, they don't look as though they've been scrubbed, now do they!'

On Middle Street there were houses on both sides, I don't know why they had to knock them down, they were lovely stone cottages. They were two bedrooms up and a kitchen and that down, a toilet down the yard and ash pits were just bricks with no cover on. Makes you wonder about hygiene in those days.

A.W.

Milk Round

When I left school we had the farm and I took a little milk round and delivered milk with buckets and a bicycle. I had to put the bucket handle to one side or my knee would catch it. Everyone in Bolsover could tell you about Bessie on a bike! One bucket held four gallons and the other two; that way you were better balanced.

Bessie Holmes

More Tinsleys

I had a great uncle Edwin Tinsley who was a loco driver and one day he had a drop too much to drink. He was late setting off from Manchester because he'd been in the pub too long and when he got down to London he was twenty minutes early. He'd never stopped anywhere and went straight through the signals!

Great uncle Charlie was a jolly, red-faced chap. He lived across at Pond House on Welbeck Road and liked nothing better than a good punch up. One night he'd been in a fight, was locked out and had to sleep in the cow shed. He caught pneumonia and died.

Most of my great uncles were farmers, some well off, some not so. One day uncle Joe met Dr Saville who gave him a frock coat as uncle's looked a bit tatty. So, at night he'd go out in this coat and a top hat so he was given the name 'Doctor' Tinsley. Some years ago someone in Palterton was telling me that relations from Gainsborough were travelling down Welbeck Road and just as they reached Pond House saw a figure in a frock coat and top hat who ran into the front of the car. But there was no bump, the figure just floated over the top of the car. They stopped and got out but there was nothing there. So there we are; these people had never been to Bolsover before and knew nothing about old Joe Tinsley. They'd obviously seen his ghost.

Tuppenny was another likely lad who went shooting a lot with my grandfather and uncle Tom who then was only a young lad. Tuppenny was a little bit wild with a gun and missing a partridge shot uncle Tom in the back of the head. Tuppenny ran off and grandfather, who had a terrible temper, for the next three months sat in the window seat of the Bull with his gun, waiting for Tuppenny. The police station was across the road in those days and the sergeant told Tuppenny he would have permission to come up Bolsover and he shouldn't do so until grandfather stopped sitting in the Bull with his gun.

John Tinsley

The Brickworks

Grandfather had three brickworks and one of those was Byron Brickworks at Carr Vale. Father was the manager; he lived here during the week with his works manager and returned to Leicester on the train at weekends.

Mr Chapman the works manager lived on Castle Lane and we came here in 1916, when I was eight. The manager of Bolsover Colliery had just bought The Mount on Castle Lane when they moved him to Creswell; it was a beautiful house. Father bought it and we moved from Leicester. There was a black path where Castle Lane is now and a cinder track for a causeway. When I was married at twenty the taxi had to come up the causeway. My father loved Bolsover. He thought it was a marvellous place and was pleased to come. A lot of the bricks were used to build Carr Vale. The Back Hills at that

Bolsover Council officers at the Valley estate. Charles Margerrison and Joe Mason are third and fourth from the left.

time was flat because it was before the slip in the 1930s. The men used to play cricket on it.

Dorothy Cutts

Fred Kitchen

We knew Fred Kitchen well, a lovely man. I'll never forget when he won a Book Club Award and he had to go to Swanwick Hall and a famous person in the literary world came up from London to go and interview Fred. She was appalled with how he lived. He was a right mixture; he was gardener at Bolsover Girls' School, worked on the Land Settlement, yet he could write books. He first became popular after the violence of the war with his nice simple stories.

He used to come across to us at Christmas when we lived on Moor Lane and especially ask for the *Messiah* on record and sit there in his dirty old gardening boots, lie back and shut his eyes and that was that. He was a very good Methodist local preacher. On the settlement he wasn't a very energetic man, wasn't a neat and tidy man but he was a wonderful fellow. I remember him going to Duckmanton School when Ellis was head and talked to the kids. He eventually wrote *Goslington* which is set in Duckmanton. He'd go with the idea of talking literature and finish up with wildlife, he was an expert on that, and talk about hares and rabbits and foxes.

Ken Leaning

Mrs George Twidle and daughter Susanna at the door of 59 High Street, in the 1920s.

Moving the Conduit House

I worked on making New Station Road. It was a government scheme for those on t'dole and they borrowed me from t'council. The footpath was all wooden sleepers and I did most of t'drainage. We shifted the Cundy House from one side of t'road to t'other on wooden sleepers and only one stone ever fell off.

Joe Mason

Coal Store

It was an uphill pull from Markham to Bolsover, for the trains. I used to wave to the trains and occasionally the driver would let me have a ride. He'd pull me up on the footplate and we'd ride on the line. All the railwaymen in the cottages had to buy their own coal, unlike the miners who got concessionary. So, what they would do when they were driving the coal train was to throw lumps down the banking as they travelled up the line. When they went off duty they walked back down to collect it.

Jack Elliot

In Service

I left school when I was twelve and stayed home for five years to look after my baby brother. Then I went into service in Nottingham. I was paid 15s a month. All the girls in my class went into service and the boys down the pit. My mother's creed was to get away and serve your betters. You came home once a year, for a week in the summer. You couldn't get home at Christmas. You got board and lodging but had to pay for

Clearing the snow from Palterton Lane during the Depression, 1933.

your own uniform. I have worked for 'proper people' and know the difference.

Ethel Hodkin (recorded 1973)

From Sutton to Bolsover

I was born at 59 High Street, Bolsover, on the site of which the Catholic church of St Bernadette now stands. My grandparents, Mr and Mrs George Twidle, with their children Susannah and William, came to live at 59 High Street from Deepdale Farm, Sutton, Scarsdale, in about 1914. Perhaps it was because Scarsdale was part of the superb view from both the house and garden that they chose this house. My grandfather had been a tenant farmer, but became ill with pernicious anaemia, and was unable to continue work on the farm.

When he came to Bolsover he bought a bus, which he housed in the garage and which my Uncle Bill drove. I believe it was the first service to run from Bolsover and I am told it was like a taxi, leaving its intended route to serve the needs of passengers. Before the Catholic church was built, the garage was used as a temporary church and the statue of St Bernadette stands in a niche made in the end of the building.

Margaret Utridge

CHAPTER 5
At Home

Food was one of the prime focus points of home life. Woodhead's shop in the Market Place provided the Bolsover housewife with the widest choice of provisions.

Anne Barfoot and cousin Derek Green in Oxcroft Lane, sitting on the bumper of one of William Barfoot's lorries.

Primitive Conditions

Outside Railway Cottages we had, under the bridge, a rising spring. You went down some wooden steps and filled up the bucket under the bridge. That was all the drinking water we had, lovely spring water it was. Washing water was collected from tanks five foot high, at the side of the house. At the other side were earth closets which the council emptied twice a year, except for ours which my dad used on the garden. He dug great trenches down the garden and filled them with lime and sewage. He grew the finest peas around but when people knew where they came from, they didn't want any!

Jack Elliot

Children's Fashions

My mother had her own dressmaker and a 'Spirella' corset lady. So I had lovely made dresses too, of lovely materials such as 'Tobrolca'. I had navy blue knickers with a pocket in the leg which always had unreliable elastic, and long black stockings which usually had a potato in the leg where I fell. These were held up by suspenders dangling from a liberty bodice. I longed for summer and white socks inside dainty black patent shoes or plimsolls.

Betty Hunter

No 'Mod Cons'

In the 1930s, my grandmother's home in Town End only had oil lamps and candles upstairs. On the other side of the mantelpiece in the sitting room there were gas lamps but that was the only power in the house. Heating and cooking were done through a black lead range. The contrast with my parents' house on Welbeck Road where we had things like a telephone, a car, electricity and a Hoover was enormous. It was spanning two centuries really.

Pam Ashley

Poverty

There was a boot and shoe fund and clothes were passed around. We were a big family and mother was an invalid. She was always in bed with rheumatoid arthritis so we had to pay for a maid, a night nurse and all the doctor's bills because there was nothing then to cover illness. So we weren't very well off either.

Joyce Leaning

Market Stalls

I can remember there used to be some market stalls at the bottom of Kitchen Croft. I can remember the flares on the stalls and I used to think, I'm sure they're a bit dangerous. Later, the stalls were in the market place and the buses and the vans used to be at the front where all the bus shelters are now and the stalls at the back. The boys used to go to the back of the butcher's stalls where the women stood – and they were all 'bonny'. These lads used to go with a pin; they found it very inviting!

Bessie Holmes

The Pearce Family

The Pearce family on High Street consisted of four brothers and sisters; Mary, Charles, Elizabeth and John. Old John Pearce owned an awful lot of land in Bolsover but when it came to paying his land tax he only paid 3s and 1s for a house! They were big church people. Charles was a bit simple. John was a magistrate. Their house on High Street, where Pearce Trust Bungalows are now, was very beautiful but those four were the last of the line and when they died the house was demolished, late in the 1930s I think. They owned a lot of farm property on High Street and land off the Clowne Ramper Road. Charles gardened some of the High Street land.

Ethel Hodkin

The Family

Mother was a dressmaker and seemed to spend a lot of her time making clothes for us. Sometimes I can see very clearly – a Buchanan tartan kilt hanging up against a glass cupboard – and a white talralco dress printed with natural-looking sprays of buttercups. She once made bridesmaids' dresses for the wedding of the daughter of the family who kept the Bluebell. There were six dresses, in sweet-pea colours.

Father was out a lot. He worked at the Bolsover Colliery Company offices and was assistant organist at the Congregational church. He also sang in the choir and was a very keen hockey player in winter and tennis player in summer, so that I hardly ever remember him being there, except at meal times. He very much enjoyed his motorcycle.

Granny seemed always to be busy about the house but she also had a lot of time for us. I liked to spend a lot of time with her in the kitchen. She was very welcoming to all who called to see her and had a very generous and warm nature and I felt very near to her. She was always very interested in what we were doing and made paper kites for us to fly in the garden.

Grandpa spent much of his time by the fireside or, in good weather, at the bottom of the garden. He was frequently in pain and was extremely thin which made it necessary for him to sit on an air-ring cushion. I was a little nervous of him at times. Sometimes he would leave his ring at the bottom of the garden and ask me to fetch it for him and I felt I must get there and back with it before he reached his fireside chair. I think illness must have made him somewhat serious, although I remember him with affection and he could be very kind. Peter and I once arrived home from school wearing team bands, both having been made team-leaders on the same day. Grandpa was delighted and gave us both a shilling.

Margaret Utridge

Harold Utridge with his wife (*née* Susannah Twidle) and children, Peter and Margaret.

Grocery Selling

My maternal grandfather, Walter George Evans, was licensee of the White Swan until 1903. He lost money in the Mansfield new cinema project. In 1906 he owned four shops in Town End and lived at the rear of them. My father, Alfred Bennet, eventually bought this property off his father and in 1930 he moved in. My mother, Eliza Ann, myself and sister Ida who was nineteen minded the grocery business. The other shops were leased to Meadow Dairy, Mr Lee the gent's outfitter and Smith, the electrician.

Trade was very poor during the Depression years of the 1930s. In

The Market Place on a cold winter's day in the 1940s. In those days the open market was still held here.

addition to the shop my father farmed ten acres of land at Pump Farm, Woodthorpe, where he was tenant to the Duke of Devonshire. He cycled there every day and stayed until milking in the evening. The potatoes, green vegetables, fowls and eggs all went into the shop to sell. An orchard provided fruit.

My mother bought other goods from Shentall's warehouse in Chesterfield and I remember going to that exciting place to order goods and pay the bills. A lot of produce was seasonal; Christmas dates which come in a block, to be chiselled out, round tips of grapes, mandarins, lemons, Seville oranges, and nuts in bags; I remember cracking these with a flat iron. Crates of oranges for Shrove Tuesday were delivered and the orange boxes were made into furniture

for the very poor. Fruit was a luxury at this time, beyond the ordinary worker, and was often only had at Christmas.

Betty Hunter

Wash Day

When I got married we had a rubber-rollered mangle, two zinc tubs and a rubbing board, which our David used eventually for his skiffle group at chapel. When we had baked bread at home I had to go home from school to help bake bread in a big brown pancheon. Youngsters today are wanting to start where it took us fifty years to reach.

A.W.

92

Wash days were very busy days. We used to start at six o'clock and had to pump the water and fill the copper with soft water from the pump. Well, it was quite a long way to carry the buckets of water and we'd light the copper fire as hot as we could, get started and we'd be washing the whole day through. Then at night we'd mangle the dry clothes, and start the ironing. It would be ten o'clock at night when we'd done. On bad days mother would have to have another fire and we'd drape clothes about and turn and turn them until they got dry eventually.

Farmers would work out in the wet in those days so all their overcoats got very wet and there weren't any tarpaulin coats in those days so they'd to be dried as well as your washing. One of the things that farmers used to wear a lot was a sack, proper sack material which they used to put corner to corner making a hood, and tie the ends together with binder twine, so that it covered shoulders and back.

When we were ironing we had to have three flat irons on a trivet on the fire, but you knew you couldn't finish a garment with one hot iron because it soon cooled off and you had to rub them with cloth to get the smoke off. It was quite an ordeal ironing. Today, I think some of the young ones would think it all a fairy story.

Ellen Spray

Outside the Bennets' shop, Town End, 1930. Left to right: Sarah Ann Evans from Pump Farm, Woodthorpe; Ida Bennet; Kathleen Bennet; young Betty Bennet.

housekeeper to the vicar who lived there. He was born in the room with the only wooden floor in the Castle. His mother, the housekeeper, I remember once had to cater for twelve curates for tea; they had a barrel of beef – whatever a barrel was!

Bessie Holmes

Born in Bolsover Castle

Both brothers were born in the Castle. My grandfather was fourteen when he left; their mother was the

Cooking by Coal

You see we used to have a coal allowance; there was no problem with coal as it was part of dad's wages.

The miller's family: Kitty Bagshaw, Mrs Bagshaw and Elizabeth Bagshaw on holiday in the 1920s.

There was always plenty of slack. Dad used to bank the fire up each night with a mug full of water on top of that and t'fire was in when they got up next morning, and that's how they would cook shin meat and anything which needed cooking all night.

A.W.

The Miller's Family

We originated from Scarcliffe. We farmed at Scarcliffe Manor next to the church and came here to the mill across the way in 1886. My grandmother lived on High Street. She was a Twidle and her people were tea merchants. I've heard mother talk about grandfather going down to the docks. He went by coach and had a blunderbuss which we had hanging on the wall and they collected crates of tea and made it up into packets. So he was a tea merchant actually but my grandfather's side were always farmers.

Marl House in those days was all one then, but of course, there were eight of us children so we needed a big house. We had two staircases, one at the front and one at the back, four big bedrooms, no bathroom, a kitchen and a room which we called the parlour which was a dining room and then what we called the drawing room in those days which ran the whole length at the front. We used to have parties, roll back the carpets and invite friends. We were members of the castle tennis club and we had dances.

We came to this house (on Welbeck Road) in 1929. An uncle had the four houses built and then this for himself, but never came here, it was let. My father sold the mill and house for £800. I was away in Ashbourne, so I didn't really miss it, but my sister did. She didn't like living here. Marl House was too big. Father died, uncle John died, grandma died, so there was only my mother and my sister Kit and it was really too big for them so we came here.

Ada Bagshaw

Night Soil

I was born in the Model Village and there were no water toilets. At the bottom of the yard there were brick buildings where you sat on a wooden plank and once a fortnight, late at night, a horse and cart would come round and you'd hear a swishing sound!

The council would be in touch with a local farmer or market gardener and they'd put it on the land as fertilizer. When I bought this house I got a three-acre field for a garden and next door the farmer had the night soil from Scarcliffe and I remember saying to him, 'Look, I'm sorry but I don't want this stuff next to my garden,' and in the end I went to the Medical Officer of Health and he had it stopped.

Ken Leaning

Bolsover in the 1950s

We moved to Bolsover in late 1953 and a couple of years later I joined the WI. They held a garden party on High Street and so I was so staggered by the view from the back that I went

Mrs Bagshaw at Filey, shortly before the First World War.

home to Charles and said there was only one place to live in Bolsover and that was High Street. In 1959 the people who lived in the cottage at the back of number 49 moved to a council house. The cottage wasn't suitable but Mrs Prosser who lived in the big house was dying to get into a flat so we bought the house. Much of High Street was being demolished. We had a highly efficient sanitary inspector; there were no grants, and health regulation applied to really old properties as well and meant that they had to come down. The old Manor House went and the cottage at the back of here which was sixteenth-century. There was a beautiful Georgian house where Pearce's bungalows are now and another three of exceptional calibre. They were all originally farms with labourers' cottages alongside and blacksmiths, shops, barns and cow houses adjoining.

When we came the cottages now restored on Cotton Street were at the back side of a yard with other buildings in front and a wonderful row of cottages across the top where the car park is now. The tithe barn at the top of Cotton Street had been a school where you paid one penny a week. The Elder Citizens' Centre had been the site for barns and farm buildings and there was a long row of cottages on High Street, opposite to where the Sportsdrome is now. All of them had wells. The Sportsdome was like an army hut then, used for boxing. End on to that was Barfoot's farmhouse; they also had a café.

On Cotton Street there was Joe Hardwick's shop, Shentalls and then Miss Weston on the corner. Fronting the market place Dennis Riley's was then a large house, one side being the Trustee Savings Bank and Ron Chambers lived in the other. Then the archway to Woodhead's shop had been filled in for Loreen Woodhouse's college library, which was a subscription library. This was followed by Mrs Eyres and Jack Eyres on the corner.

Bunty Margerrison

Village Shops

There were three shops in Palterton, a general grocer, a post office and a sweet shop which also sold bits and bobs – all sorts of things. One was a lock-up wooden shop and a Miss Spray, no relation to us, lived there. I remember once looking in the windows longingly at this doll dressed in red and I wrote a letter to Santa Claus. Anyway, I got this doll and I've got it to this day. It's broken now but it's travelled from one room to another all its life.

Ellen Spray

Visitors

It was a long time before I understood why the window cleaner gave money to Granny. He arrived frequently, not just to clean windows, and handed over money which was put into a tall lidded pewter pot above the fireplace. I learnt years later that Granny was his banker. He lodged in a house in High Street and would bring his earnings for Granny to keep for him so that he would not spend it all at the Bluebell, and so have his rent available each weekend. I think it was probably just once during each summer that Bob Banner would come bringing a magnificent bunch of mixed flowers from his garden.

Every Sunday, or so it seemed to me, Uncle Bill's friend, an AA man, would roar into the yard with his shiny yellow motorcycle and sidecar.

We liked to hear the shout 'Ice Creamayi!' which heralded the arrival of Mr Cutts at the front door. He pushed a cart in which a zinc tub bobbed about in a sea of chunks of ice. He dug into the tub with a wooden spatula and piled up delicious yellow ice-cream into cornets which stood like little towers in the corner of the cart, or else would spread it into a pop-up wafer-

Flecknell's shop in the old Market Place at the turn of the century.

maker for the grown-ups.

The scissors-grinder also came regularly, wheeling his cart to the front door and calling out for work.

Margaret Utridge

Basics

We had oil lamps, no electricity or running water. I was married in the 1940s before I had a flush toilet or a bathroom.

Jack Elliot

Great Uncle

My great uncle lived at 'Dane Bank', that's Woodhouse's shop, and my mother used to tell me that in the front room they had suits of armour. He had quite a bit of money and horses and carriages. They were gentry I suppose. My grandfather had a bit of land up Steel Lane and Elmton Lane and he got himself a tin bungalow from somewhere and he used to work with wood so he lined the floors and walls and they lived up Steel Lane in this bungalow. His wife used to drink gin and go in the Swan next door. She used to go and tuck it under her dress. When her husband found out one day he horse-whipped her and then my grandfather took the whip and whipped him.

Bessie Holmes

Before the curtain rises at the Assembly Hall in the 1940s. The lack of aisles and densely packed seating leads you to wonder what they would have done in a fire.

Local Shops

Often I would go out with my mother to shop at the little grocer's at the top of Cotton Street. The row of terraced houses where the shop was has been pulled down. Mrs Guntrip's shop was entered up steep stone steps and was kept by an ever-smiling Mrs Guntrip who stood behind a little counter to the right as one entered. It used to seem that the shop was packed with goods from floor to ceiling. She would weigh out yeast – or balm as we used to call it – from a hessian bag into a shining brass scale-pan, and used little brass weights, and served tub-butter from a great block into crackling greaseproof paper. The shelf above the window had a row of

exciting and colourful glass jars full of boiled sweets and there was always a box of liquorice laces and coils of liquorice with sweets in the centre around the shop.

I liked to go to buy biscuits from Shentalls or Woodheads. They were packed in tilted cubed-shaped tins with glass hinged lids, so that the contents could be viewed. Pink wafer biscuits looked especially inviting. Sometimes we bought Cadbury's Cup Chocolate in very pretty paper covered cartons. They were a beautiful blue, patterned with pairs of ladies and gentlemen in powdered wigs and pretty costumes, amongst a pattern of flowers. On very special occasions I remember a rather special wrapped chocolate wafer biscuit being bought, which I think was called De Beaukeler.

A visit to Mr Blant's toyshop in the Market Place was always interesting. He sold fascinating clockwork toys and dolls. The Friday markets, which were at the time held in the Market Place, provided lovely remnants which were made into pretty dresses and blouses.

When mother went to Chesterfield I used to like to run along High Street watching her when she appeared at the top of Cotton Street. She would come home with treats from Woolworths, such as a new arrival for the farm and I remember being very pleased with a cardboard bathroom completely fitted with china bath, wash basin and lavatory, with a doll to scale.

Margaret Utridge

Early Buses

We had few buses. Underwoods connected Bolsover with Mansfield and Flint's ran to Shirebrook. They were dreadfully smelly buses and I was always sick. Route 3B ran to Shuttlewood and Bentinck only. We had to walk from Woodthorpe Farm and I always remember that or riding on the cross bar of my father's push bike.

Betty Hunter

The Privy

In the Castle Street house, down the garden were two toilets side by side, each of them double. One double was for adult and child, the other for two adults. They were emptied weekly and Auntie Esther remembers the smell as being horrible.

Anne Joyce

Balloon Swallowing

On Fridays we used to have a halfpenny or a penny and go round one or two of the sweet shops to see where we could get most for the money. Next to Harrison's there was a tuck shop and Edwin went in and said he was going to have Spanish juice with a balloon on the end of it. Anyway, we came out of the shop and Edwin went off crying like billy-oh and I ran after him and caught him up on Welbeck Road. He said, 'I've swallowed my balloon!' We went home to father and he said, 'You've done it now, your mother's not in, she's gone to market. You'd better go find her.' So we went and he kept saying to me, 'I shan't die, Bessie, shall I?' 'Oh no,' I said, 'everybody swallows balloons,' but I was really worried to death. Anyway, mother went home post-haste and took him to see Dr Stratton. She was in a real old sweat. Dr Stratton said to give him two ounces of castor oil and a dry biscuit, which she did and then put us to bed. But she never slept. Anyway, it came up during the night. Fortunately it had gone down the right way. If it had filled up with air, he couldn't have breathed. He never ever blew up a balloon after that, not even at Christmas.

Bessie Holmes

Chairman of the Coal Board Sir Hubert Houldsworth and Lady Houldsworth (right) examine the 'Lamp of Flowers' at New Bolsover Village Hall, November 1953. Cllr Sid Fisher, chairman of Bolsover UDC, and Mrs Fisher (left) are hosts.

Milk Pudding

Milk itself was delivered to the door in a great big pan and ladled out. The dairy down Carr Vale was called Clement's and if mother wanted to make a rice pudding it was 'just nip round to Clement's and bring me a quart of skimmed milk.' The rice was washed and rinsed through a colander and then a little drop of water. I can see my mother doing it now; to cree she used to call it. That would go into the oven at a very low heat; she wouldn't mend t'fire until all the water was absorbed by the rice, then it would come out and it had a sprinkle of salt on it, all the quart of milk, a knob of butter and sugar, then it was put in the oven all day. It was a lovely rice pudding.

A.W.

Peg Rugs

Mother said we would have some doormats so we had to make one each, all five children. These were peg rugs mother made out of knitted skirts and suits or a vest which she'd dyed, and before she died, she made all of her grandchildren make one. We used to have what you call congolium squares and they only cost two shillings. They were squares of very cheap linoleum to look like carpet.

Ellen Spray

Scrumping

We had an orchard and we children used to go scrumping and my elder brother, he was very quiet but full

100

of mischief in a quiet sort of way, and he'd say, 'I'll show you how to bury them in a haystack to keep, and when you want one you just come and get it.' But the thing was when he went back to look for them, he couldn't find them! Mother made jelly with the fruit and but it was an old orchard and the fruit was small. We also made pickles, chutney and lots and lots of jam. There was always plenty of home-made stuff, in fact that's what you had.

We had the big black stove with the open fire and the hob at one side with water in and mother had enormous big iron saucepans. Empty they were heavy – oh they were awful! And she'd have three pans wedged somehow on the fire, especially on Sundays. We had potatoes in one and carrots or winter turnips in another. There were no packets of frozen peas in those days. I used to wonder how she'd concoct that lovely dinner with roast beef and Yorkshire pudding and yet it was so difficult; wonderful really.

Ellen Spray

Candle Power

Auntie's cottage on Town End had no running water or electricity. Upstairs there were feather beds and you went upstairs with a candle. They had a stone sink but all the water came from an outside well. This would be in the 1930s, but it could have been the 1830s.

Pam Ashley

Wash Day Pudding

It was my job to clean t'kitchen floor. Dad used to fill the copper and it was a full day's job to heat it. My brother used to mangle t'clothes and me and my sister had to help with t'ironing with flat irons. To dry things we had a big wooden clothes horse round the fire. There was steam everywhere and mother used to make a bit of a meat hash and 'wash day pudding' – a slice of bread and jam with milk poured on it.

A.W.

Long Lives

My eldest sister would have been ninety-nine. I'm ninety-four. Another sister in Chesterfield is ninety-two. My sister in the home is ninety and I lost another last October, and she was eighty-nine.

Ada Bagshaw

Palterton Hall

The hall is not really as big as it looks. There are two windows to each room, very big rooms and very high. There were two main bedrooms which were large; 15ft square. There were two master bedrooms, two back ones, one of which father made into a bathroom, and then two more 15ft square rooms; eight bedrooms in all, but some only used as storerooms. It was very cold in winter but you grew up with it. We took some stone hot water bottles to bed or mother would put a brick in the oven and wrap it up in cloth and occasionally she'd wrap the oven shelf in it and let you take that upstairs. You grew up with that coldness.

Ellen Spray

Christmas Time and Mummers

Christmas was an exciting time. Mother and granny would make several hampers to send away to relations and we helped in the stirring of the mincemeat and puddings. The postman would arrive with intriguing parcels and I remember one specially exciting parcel which arrived from auntie Emily in Liverpool, which contained amongst other things a beautiful pair of green shoes for me.

A Christmas tree which reached the ceiling was in our living room and was lit by candles in clip-holders. Decorations included birds with spun glass tails, a trumpet, a beautiful china fairy on the top. Five, or was it seven, china cherubs with glass wings 'flew' on the tree.

I think it would be on Boxing Day or maybe the day after, that Mrs Bagguley would bring her family to a party. We used to play a game which I have never heard of anyone else playing. My father would lay down with a coat covering him and at his head was a pair of shoes and at his feet, a hat. Each child was invited to the hat end and when no reply came, encouraged to bend lower as 'he' couldn't hear. Eventually, Father, rolled paper in hand would sit up and suddenly wallop the seat of the bending child. It seemed quite marvellous that after being surprised once in this way,

anyone would play again, but we played it year after year.

One Christmas stays very clear in my memory. We were sitting having our dinner in our living room when I asked for more trifle. Mother said I could go down to granny in the kitchen to get some so I took my dish and opened the door and as I did so I saw pairs of eyes shining out of black faces and heard unknown voices in the darkness. I fled back into the room, crying and ran into my mother's arms, followed by the team of mummers who had come to give a performance. I vaguely remember them acting and I think it might have been St George and the Dragon, but I had received such a shock that I was still afraid.

Margaret Utridge

Home Memories

I dimly remember the old market place and the stalls with hissing lamps on rainy nights. People shopped late as they were not paid until Friday teatime when there was last minute haggling for cheap meat and perishables. I played under the street gas light on Town End, with light reflected from the shop, until hauled in protestingly by the parents.

I spent my halfpenny at Hinde's shop, what is now Marple's, and could linger over a choice of Tiger nuts, liquorice wood which was chewed until it hung in shreds, aniseed balls, bullseyes which changed colour or sherbet dips. I later transferred my allegiance to Grocott's sweet shop opposite where a friend lived.

Behind our shop was a lovely walled

Bolsover Great Central Line station in the 1890s.

garden. My grandfather was a good gardener. There was a lawn, roses, apple trees and purple flagstones under an ivy-covered wall. Outside we also had a water closet and coal shed. Inside the house we had gas mantles but candles in the bedrooms in the early days. Four large bedrooms faced Town End which had coal fires. When we were ill I remember my father carrying red hot coals up the stairs to get it started. Downstairs, we had a coal range with oven and a water boiler, on at each side. In front was a brass fender. I always remember that bed warmers were a hot oven shelf, a heated brick, or stone water bottles.

The scullery had a stone sink and was donkey stoned. In the sitting room there was a large leather horsehair sofa and on one wall stood a large mahogany dresser with a set of large carved mirrors. On the top was displayed a large brass tea urn, resplendent with handles and a tap. Also, a Georgian silver teapot presented

to my father from the pigeon club at the Nags Head at Palterton dating from the time he was licensee there during the First World War.

Betty Hunter

Family Life

When my father came home from Chesterfield my brother would say, 'Have you brought us any sweets, dad, anything from Woolies?' 'Aye, look in your mother's bag,' and there was always something, a notebook or a pencil from the penny bazaar. Then the sweets would come out. He'd tip them out onto a serviette and we'd all have the same amount and if there was one over he'd keep it for himself and say, 'That's for me because I'm t'sergeant!' Our Sunday morning breakfast, every week before we went to Sunday School, I had at my grandmother's because she'd have meat stewing all day; shin beef and gravy. It was great.

A.W.

Mealtimes

On Friday night the range fire was made up and shin beef was put in a casserole overnight. It was a most flavoursome Saturday breakfast. Sunday was joint day with a large sirloin leg of lamb or pork from Watson's butchers. We had cold meat off the bone for Sunday supper with pickles and home-made bread. Monday breakfast was toast and dripping with meat jelly from the joint. Father always enjoyed a steak in the evening, fried over the coal fire and with home grown vegetables. Washday Monday meant cold meat and a fry up of leftover Sunday veg.

Betty Hunter

Farmhouse Cooking

We used to kill our own pig and salt it on a salting stone down the cellar and then hang it and dry it on the hooks. The big hams were rubbed with saltpetre and cured beautifully. You could have one for two or three years and it would still be good. At Christmas mother would get father to unhook it and get it down. He would cut a lovely piece out, cover it up with muslin and she'd boil it. It had to be soaked for twelve hours to get the salt out. It was lovely. Mother would make about twenty pork pies and although there were no fridges we kept eating them until they were done and we never seemed to be harmed by it. We'd give some away and she'd make them of different sizes. They looked lovely on the table.

We'd make our own butter and mother would get me to turn the churn handle. Oh that was chronic to a child, turning for an hour, and when she wasn't looking I'd turn like mad but that was silly because the cream wasn't moving. There was a little window you'd look through and that had to be clear before it was ready. She'd make a design on the top with 'Scotch Hands' that you'd pat it with and she had a few customers that liked it.

My mother also made very nice cheese. She'd cut the curd down and then across into cubes. She'd place it in a big ring and put a board on top with a lot of weights and let it mature perhaps three weeks and you'd eat them in turn. We had to be flush with milk for mother to do that.

Ellen Spray

Caravan Life

When we got married we went to Gordon Lamb's and bought a caravan which we had in the farm yard and we lived there for eighteen years. Happy as pigs in muck we were.

Bessie Holmes

Bath Night

We used to bath in front of the fire in those days. It was a right rigmarole; getting in the hot water in an old-fashioned black range with a boiler at the side. I can remember having to black-lead it; there was the oven at one side and the boiler at the other and just in the middle was a recess that we used to put plates in.

A.W.

Left: Mrs Twidle in the 1890s, aged thirty-four years.
Right: Mr George Twidle of the High Street, in the 1890s.

Illness Remedies

Dr Lane Snr had his surgery on Langwith Road. He lived on Hill Top and was a kind, fatherly, jovial man, a good friend to many. We used to sell him boiling fowls for his growing family. We had to pay for doctor's visits in those days.

I remember having to wear Thermogene Chest Protectors which you plucked off gradually. When spring came, there was goose grease and Vic for your chest. Popular remedies were lime and sulphur tablets, Fenning's Fever Cure, linseed and bread poultices and syrup of figs. Iodine came in a ribbed dark bottle, as did all poisons.

Betty Hunter

59 High Street

If one did not turn along the left-hand passage, the kitchen was reached. This was a very welcoming room. It had a Yorkshire range where, I think, a fire always glowed. The high mantelpiece held interesting pieces of china and pewter and the large deal table was usually covered by a dark cloth. A sofa was behind the table and above this, a corner cupboard hung, out of which little treats were taken. A large stone sink to the right of the fireplace had a hand pump beside it and the window above.

Across the passage was the dairy. This had stone slabs, underneath which were pancheons and a cream-jar which had come from the farm. There were hooks in the ceiling for hams, but I don't think they were used except for poultry. A large round hip-bath with a high back and 'wings' for soap hung on the wall. I think it must have been made of papier mâché as it was not heavy. The outside was biscuit-coloured and the inside white. It was put in front of the kitchen fire for baths and filled with hot water from the boiler at the side of the fire, after we children became too big to be bathed in the metal bath which would stand in the sink. There was also a meat safe in the dairy and jugs of milk were covered with circles of net or crochet, round which glass beads were stitched to weight the edges.

I remember only a little about the upstairs part of the house. All the windows had creaky shutters and one could kneel in the windows and look down into the street. Once, late at night, performing bands from the castle went in procession along High Street and members of one band had lights on their hats and costumes.

I recollect a rather beautiful and unusual wallpaper in my parents' bedroom, glade with roses in shades of perile, and a high-sided cot at the side of their bed which I found I could somersault, making a soft landing. My brother Philip was born in that room three months before we left High Street.

There were a number of outhouses, one of which housed two earth closets, side by side, and another similar building was used by the smithy. In the garden was the top of a train which had been made into two rooms which was put there for my uncle. Uncle Bill had one undeveloped lung and on medical advice, my grandparents sought to give him an open-air environment. It wasn't used in my lifetime except as a playroom. The walls were panelled in wood and it was my delight to find blisters which had been raised by the sun on the varnished surface. These could be pressed and cracked leaving creamy coloured egg-shapes on the walls.

On either side of the train were areas of garden in which clumps of flowers grew. I clearly remember oriental poppies. These two small gardens had fences either side of the train, cutting them off from the rough meadow grass area in the middle. Behind the garage was a small kitchen garden.

The low stone wall at the bottom of the garden had large stones which jutted out from the wall's surface on which one could sit and enjoy the view. Just below the wall was a path running the length of the back-hills. There was also, and still is, what is now known to be a conduit tower, but was then thought to be a watch tower and we imagined a look-out being kept across the valley for the approach of enemies on their way back to attack the castle.

The house was entered from the street through a porch and our living room was on the left at the bottom of the stairs. It was a square room with a window seat and fireplace above which were brass gas-mantle brackets. The piano had hinged fittings for candles. On some evenings, granny would come in and play and sing Victorian ballads, like 'Just a song at twilight' and my father often played.

Opposite the window was a cupboard with glass-panelled sliding doors which filled the whole of the wall. I think it was put in when my mother and father married and seemed to hold most of our

Lady Edwina Mountbatten meets the St John Ambulance Brigade Ladies' Section at New Bolsover, September 1955.

possessions.

A long stone-flagged corridor ran from the front door through to the back of the house. Opening from it on the right was the living room which Uncle Bill and Auntie May and, later, Alison lived in, until they moved to the Model Village. I remember only once going into that room to see my only cousin Alison, as a baby.

Down the passage and to the left was a shorter passage leading to what we used to call 'the blackcock room'. They were not in fact cockroaches which inhabited this spare room, but rain-beetles. The room, which was at one time a doctor's waiting room had double doors opening into the garden under which insects were prone to crawl. It was slightly damp and cold and had various cases and boxes stored in it, which, when moved, usually sent one or two beetles or spiders scurrying away.

For this reason I viewed the room with some fear and hoped never to be sent to fetch anything from it.

Margaret Utridge

CHAPTER 6

Wartime

Winifred, Duchess of Portland, opening a garden party at Sherwood Lodge in aid of the National Air-
Raid Distress Fund in 1942. Joyce Day remembers the Duchess' face as 'looking like an enamel mask'.

A 'Bolsover Jams' promotion in the 1950s.

Life in 'Dad's Army'

I was the headmaster of the National School during the war years and for teachers over a certain age teaching was regarded as a reserved occupation. The Local Defence Volunteers were formed in 1940, everybody and anybody put their names down and rotas were drawn up to look out for the enemy. There was no equipment whatsoever. The castle was the HQ with Barfoot's shop as a sort of office to begin with and the National School was used for meetings. After a while it was realized that inland at least, the LDV wasn't going to achieve anything so the Home Guard was formed and some equipment provided. Many old soldiers from the first war signed on at the council offices in Cotton Street. We had drill parades and

met in the castle grounds, the school hall or the riding school. There was also a small shooting range in the Terrace range.

I became company commander of 'A' Company, the 5th Derbyshire Home Guard Battalion. 'A' company was Bolsover and stretched from Glapwell to Stanfree. 'B' company was Langwith and Shirebrook. There were five platoons in this area with a combined strength of 550 men; eighty-five per cent were equipped with rifles, sten guns and bayonets. We had machine guns or Lewis guns, the old standby from the First World War. People like Tom Fulleylove knew these items backwards. The only military experience was at teacher training college when I was a member of the Officers' Training Corps. My rank in the Home Guard was Major.

Two assistant company commanders were Captains. Arnold Noble was platoon commander for the castle platoon, based at Barfoot's shop and the castle was company HQ until the drill hall on Moor Lane was built. Platoons were also based at Glapwell and Hillstown Miners' Welfare. Pat Jennings was based at Bainbridge Hall. There was also one at the Coalite plant which met at the works. Oxcroft platoon was for the pit and based on the Miners' Welfare. Here, all the men were already employed but eventually we had Lillian Jennings as full-time typist, a captain quartermaster and two PT instructors. We also had some older men who had been in the guards; Harry Rhodes and Arnold Noble were quiet and steady, knowing all the military stuff backwards and they were good with the men. I was also allowed a couple of part time clerks. We were out every evening and there was a lot of admin to do as they wanted all the returns on military lines.

We had no uniforms at first until they issued denim outfits which were terrible but later we became quite well equipped with lashings of ammunition, which was stored at the castle. We practised firing at Totley or Belper and constructed our own bombing range between the pit and the railway embankment, going towards the plant and a further site at Oxcroft between the tips. We got through hundreds of live bombs and never had a casualty. We also had a Smith gun which we could aim from the castle terrace towards Bolsover Hill. The objective of the Home Guard was to detect and deter the enemy until regular troops could be brought in, not fight or capture them. We were also a lookout force, every night in the castle, on a two-hour shift basis. We did this in twos but one night I had to do it alone. I had to walk in the pitch black from the keep gate, across the courtyard, let myself in the keep, across the dining hall, lock it up and then go up the stairs, right to the top. Until I reached the battlements and the open air, I was frightened to death!

Jack Radford had just finished living in the castle then, as custodian. He was a dwarf with a humped back and his wife was a local teacher. His language was 'colourful' and often I'd come out of school with Jack bellowing at some lads for trespassing in the castle. I kept him sweet by leaving him half a pint at the Angel each day. One day we were digging slit trenches on castle land and Jack came out swearing. David Brightmore who was down the trench looked up and said 'Jack, we're digging thy bloody grave!' He regarded the castle as handed to him personally by the Duchess of Portland. Duchess Winifred used to come and visit him and he'd touch his forelock all the way round the castle.

Life in the Home Guard worked through humour and comradeship. If it hadn't been like that, after a day's shift at the colliery men wouldn't have come. If you weren't fighting overseas through being in a reserved occupation like mining there was a moral pressure to defend which was backed up with military authority, although I don't remember it coming to that here.

There were exercises and once we had to take the police station at Brimington Road. We attacked over the fields across Calow and Tapton. They also sent a flanking column round Spital. We took the police station by

The stone cottages still remain on Cotton Street, but in a much more open setting.

9.30 a.m. on Sunday morning and although there was no element of surprise, umpires were appointed to assess your capabilities. There was no transport. We were purely infantry. We always provided our own refreshment and fuel for the castle which at night was extremely cold. You were given a full uniform, gaiters, great coat, battledress, tin hat, boots and a gas mask.

For fire-watching, each street was responsible for organizing its own security, although the main urban centres like Sheffield were more centralized in their organization. ARP centres in Bolsover were the Travellers' Rest at Shuttlewood and the clinic on Welbeck Road.

The early days of the 'Dad's Army'

programmes were pretty accurate although in the early years of the war it was no laughing matter and after Dunkirk many of us thought we would become an occupied country. We were never a joke locally but many people wondered if all the intense activity was necessary.

After the end of the war, in 1946, all the records were sent to Derby for destroying and the weapons had to be accounted for. Any that weren't handed in were collected by the police, although we didn't have any trouble here.

Some Italian POWs were housed at Langwith and Southgate at Clowne. They worked on the land and at Coalite. There was a German officers' camp at the Hayes in Swanwick. They had a photo of Hitler in the dining hall and at mealtimes they all stood up and toasted him. One man did escape and was never caught. They were extremely difficult to deal with. On one occasion something upset them and they piled all the bedding on the lawns and set fire to it. Within three days it had all been replaced from Midland Draperies in Derby and at a time when such things weren't available for the British people.

If you were at the cinema and there was a warning it would be flashed on the screen 'ARP men needed'. Fires at the pit were a constant problem.

R. Fletcher

Air Raid

The only scare we had was when I was coming out of t'pit one night, about ten o'clock. We were in t'baths there, under t'showers and there was this mighty bang. We ran out and they'd dropped these bombs at Hillstown, they were just getting rid of them. They also dropped some land mines in t'fields up near Sutton Hall; I remember them going off. When they were bombing Sheffield you could hear them all that distance away and me and t'wife were at that front door many a night. There was an air-raid shelter just outside t'front door, there's a bit of a mound there now. I had the job of keeping t'key. They put a stove in and I had to put a fire in each night. But folks would say, 'Oh, they'll not catch us,' and no one used to go in and t'air raid shelter deteriorated.

Alf Bentley

Air-Raid Shelters

In the shelter we used to take a flask of tea down and there were seats each side. We were next door to the Manse and used to share it with the parson and his housekeeper. She was not posh, but very sedate and all there. She used to go into the shelter with white gloves on! Two old cousins of mother came from Leicester, two old maids. They were teachers and they went to sit under the stairs when the siren went. I remember them telling my father, 'Oh, we were quite alright, Leslie – we put the tin bath over our heads!'

Dorothy Cutts

Home Guard

I had a bicycle and with being a bugler in t'Boys' Brigade I had the job, when they were having exercises, which they had every fortnight, of having to go round all Carr Vale and t'Model Village calling: 'Fall in, March.' I had to go on t'bike with one hand. Many's a man cursed at me at six o'clock in the morning. I think that was my role in the Home Guard right up to the time he demobbed us, in front of St Winifred's church it was, two hundred or more in four rows.

Alf Bentley

Wartime Recipes

I remember mother doing something with the fat ration; the butter and margarine. She would mix it together,

By the 1920s, the Army and Navy Stores in the Old Market Place was a private house, but the sign remained. The shop front is still recognizable today.

melt it down and put milk and gelatine with it. I had to ladle this stuff into a basin and it went further but it wasn't really palatable, just something to at least put on your bread. We also used shaving soap for washing. It wasn't very effective but it did make a lather.

Marion Jones

Black Market

During the war the Mission had to be closed down and it was used as a place for air-raid wardens to meet. My husband was a special constable and he had to go out at night on his bicycle and cycle round, ensuring the blackout was kept. Farmers were better off than those on rations. We made our own butter and cheese and had turnips and potatoes and killed a pig. The only black market we had, although we didn't consider it was such, was with your personal grocer who'd pop in a few extra bits in your bag and so you would give him a bit of farm bacon or butter.

Ellen Spray

War Deaths

I remember during the First World War we all knitted socks for the men at the front. Everyone we knew was killed. All our friends as they were just that age and they all had to go. That's why many people of my age have no friends. They all died very young.

Kath Palmer

114

'Bolsover Boys Respond to the Call to Arms.' How many returned from the trenches of the Great War?

Wartime Wedding

When I was married in June 1941 we were allowed extra rations for the wedding. We had half a pound of margarine and one pound of sugar extra, so I found someone to make me a cake. You couldn't have white icing so we had to have a sort of chocolate and it was a very hot day, the day Russia came into the war; and all the chocolate and icing melted! Miners got extra cheese, they needed it. My friend Peggy Ellis had a shop on Welbeck Road and I went once a month to help count all the points, you had points for a tin of salmon for example, and all these squares had to be accounted for, and it was a job.

Joyce Leaning

Recollections of Two World Wars

I remember the men who were enlisting in the Market Place going off in an open-topped charabanc. I had a brother of course who was two years older than me. Luckily he went through the first war but he didn't survive the second. He was captured in Africa and then imprisoned in Austria and died there in a camp. To get out of the first war he went to Sheffield and passed as a wireless operator and just finished his exams when the war ended. I remember when I was teaching in Ashbourne. German POWs were billeted on an airfield and they paraded round the villages. They were all in digs and had to work on the farms. They had to be escorted of course. With rations, the only thing I really missed was sugar. Living on a farm we had eggs, cheese, butter and milk, so I was lucky.

Ada Bagshaw

A Bolsover Waterworks Committee outing. Among the officials are Drs Stratton and McKay, John Henry Adsetts, Merrill Stubbins and the Council Clerk, T.B. Kenyon.

Raids on Sheffield

The first air raid was when they bombed Sheffield. Now my sister lived in Sheffield and she was in the midst of all that. Her husband was on police watch and they spent many a night under the kitchen table.

A.W.

Bombing Duckmanton

I was teaching at Shuttlewood School and going in the shelter with the children when the sirens went, with a bucket at the end – for one hundred infants and all deciding they needed the bucket at the same time. The shelter was basically trenches and they covered them over with corrugated iron, earth and sods and we had long benches with a bucket at the end with a curtain. If you were in too long, the kiddies would get fretful and want their mum.

There was a parachute mine at Duckmanton. We could hear these planes come over, they were going to Sheffield and one of them released this mine. There was an almighty explosion, lights and so on and it demolished Duckmanton School completely but nobody was hurt. You could hear them going over to Liverpool and Manchester and you could tell it wasn't ours, there was a difference in sound.

Joyce Leaning

CHAPTER 7

Chapel and Church

The annual pantomime was one of the highlights of the chapel year and Town End, in the early 1950s, was no exception. Can you recognize Elizabeth Harrison, Janice Ogden, Margaret Travell, Jean Woodhead, Enid Kemp, Pippa Dodsworth, Gwyneth Ginnever, Margaret Wagstaffe, Rene Coalwood and Maureen Tebbs?

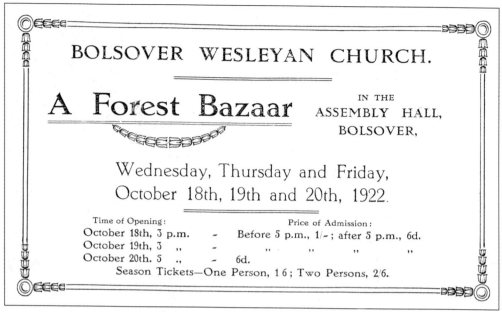

A bazaar for Hill Top Methodist church. The objective was to raise £300 for painting and renovating the church and Sunday school and to renew the heating.

Calcroft Tinsley and Hamilton Grey

Calcroft Tinsley, one of my ancestors, was vicar of Bolsover from 1810 to 1830. I was always brought up to believe he was a rum old beggar. He was supposed to have chased his wife round the castle battlements, but in fact it was she who chased him with a meat cleaver. I understand he married a daughter of Lord Frith of Chapel-en-le-Frith and she was a bit fiery. It was said he never attended church as vicar but according to Keith White, a former custodian at the castle who had consulted the records at Welbeck, the only evidence against him came from his curate Hamilton Grey. Jim Swain, former parish church organist, told me to look at the parish registers which would prove that Calcroft Tinsley was

the most maligned man in Bolsover. So I did, and it showed me that every wedding, every funeral and every birth was in Calcroft's own hand. I think he was a bit of a reprobate and he liked good spirits but there was only one signature which indicated a shaky hand through too much whisky. Hamilton Grey wanted to be vicar and live in the vicarage which in those days was the castle. I've always considered him to be a snobbish man and a bit of a bigot. He considered himself superior to the people of Bolsover. Hamilton Grey said the castle was a terrible place when he moved in when all it needed was a bit of good furniture, care and attention. The Duke of Portland, however, refused to throw Calcroft Tinsley out of the castle even when Grey took over, so the former vicar and the current one lived in the same vicarage until Hamilton Grey paid Calcroft £25, which was a lot of money in those days, to move out. They both lived in the keep and it was said Calcroft's wife would shove him through the tunnel to church, so he couldn't call in any pubs on the way. People will tell you there isn't a tunnel between castle and church but I can show you the blocked-up doorway.

John Tinsley

Chapel Organist

My father was organist at Town End chapel from 1900 to the 1950s. He played at all the weddings and funerals. He bought all the music himself and had it printed at Harold Kent's printers on Station Road. He was a night overman at the colliery for thirty years and very often there was a pit emergency. I can see my mother now, standing on the window seat in 'High Bank' on Castle Lane watching for him to come across the parks. He'd come home at midday in his pit dirt having worked since 9 p.m. the previous night. He'd get washed, go to bed and often be up at three o'clock in the afternoon to go and play for a funeral, then back to work at nine o'clock at night.

Father was one of four brothers and they were all musical. Every Christmas they'd come to our house, everyone sat round and we all had to sing, as well as singing to neighbours down Castle Lane. I joined the choir at fifteen as a soprano and then the main contralto moved out of the area so my father said, 'Right, you are now a contralto!'

Everything I value in my life came through the chapel. We held a chapel anniversary in January with a concert

Anne and David Joyce on their wedding day, the ceremony of which was held in the Cavendish chapel, as the main body of the church had been destroyed by fire.

on the Saturday and every section of the church gave an item; the Sunday school, young ladies' class, youth club and the men's group. The anniversary was the only time many kids got new clothes.

In summer there was a Sunday school party on Mill Field, up Moor Lane, and we had a tea in the Sunday school. Eric Dodsworth would come and everyone was given a bag of sweets. Looking back they were the happiest days of your life.

Marion Jones

Mrs G. Seager, president of the Women's Section at Town End Methodist chapel, presents a gift to Mrs R. Fisher on her ninetieth birthday. The Minister, Revd D.M. Clark, is to the right.

Roof-Top Greenhouse

We all went to church. Dad was a big church man, he was a sidesman and churchwarden. I was a Sunday school teacher, we were always big church people and my grandpa has a door under the organ going into the belfry which is dedicated to him. He had the post office in the Market Place, in that very large stone house, now demolished. On the roof he had a big greenhouse where he grew the most gorgeous grapes. It was actually on top of the house.

Kath Palmer

Third Time Unlucky?

David and I were married in the Cavendish chapel following the church fire in 1960. History was repeating itself because after the first fire in 1897 my grandparents also had to use the chapel because the church had burnt down. We made front page in the Derbyshire Times: 'History repeats itself for Bolsover Bride'.

When my daughter Nicola got married at the same church we were a little worried that it wouldn't burn down a third time!

Anne Joyce

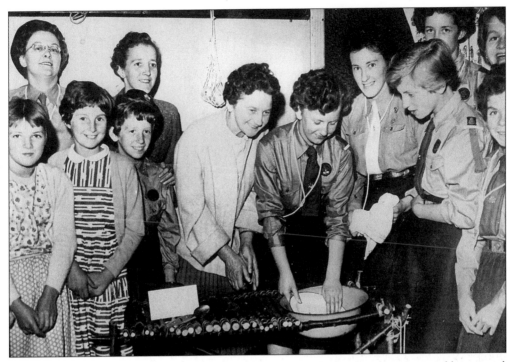

Mrs Speakman observes Bolsover Guides as they demonstrate the art of washing up in cold water and without a sink.

Chapel Life

When the Primitive Methodist chapel at Town End merged with the Wesleyans at Hill Top it took a bit of getting used to and some of them never did go. We always had big choirs at chapel and everyone belonged to the church. We had pantomimes; Mrs Wycherley would sing – she had a lovely contralto voice – and Mrs Marsh would play the piano and we had to do it just so. Mrs Goodman from Shuttlewood chapel would help us. We had operettas; oh, it all kept people together. Then we had a tennis club, up Oxcroft Lane, and we used to do a lot of hiking as we called it in those days.

A.W.

Dancing for the Bishops

I began attending the parish church before the last war when Canon Padgett was vicar, but I was too young to really remember him. George Lewis Lloyd was the earliest one I really knew as a child. Mrs Lewis Lloyd was a teacher at Tapton House. They had three children, Timothy, Gillian and Rosemary, and both the vicar and his wife were really interested in young people. She ran the Girls' Friendly Society which did an immense amount of good for local girls. Mrs Lewis Lloyd was a full time teacher and had a busy life as a vicar's wife. She employed a nanny for the children but even though very busy she still found time to spend on us. We did things like folk dancing and on one occasion were invited to

Town End chapel anniversary, early 1950s.

Lambeth Palace to dance at a Bishops' Conference. It got us country girls out and we saw things we never would have seen, especially in the early days following the war when life was very limited for most people.

Pam Ashley

Chapel Treasurer

Dad was treasurer of the chapel and he had to have the cheques signed by Mrs Sykes at Sherwood Lodge. He'd take me with him and I used to sit in the hall. There were stuffed foxes' heads on the wall and big bookcases full of things they'd brought back from their travels. Abel Charlesworth Sykes was dead when I knew her and she was an invalid like my mother so they kept in touch about their treatments. I used to go into the lovely big kitchen and the

maid would give you a buttered teacake, it was lovely. Their telephone number was Bolsover number 1. Abel Sykes gave the land for the chapel and two cottages at the side. Every year they held a strawberry tea when you were allowed to walk round the rose garden very carefully and she would come out in a wheelchair.

When I went to college she sent for me and gave me a Bible, inscribed; 'To Miss Day. Best wishes for your future and hoping you will be a blessing to many in your work.' I've still got it. She was a great benefactor to Bolsover.

Dad was on the council when they bought Sherwood Lodge and according to a lot of people, they paid too much for it. I think it was £2,800. She was very proud of the gardens and they were beautifully kept. There were two gardeners.

Joyce Leaning

Revd W. Speakman tells a story to children in their Sunday best, 1950s.

The Revd and Mrs Speakman

The Revd Speakman was a boy, he was. The thing was that if you stood up to him you were alright. I remember being asked to give a vote of thanks after one of his talks and Sheila Bagguley told me I'd disagreed with everything he said! He never really minded that but if you got his back up there was friction all the way.

Mrs Speakman was a lot younger than him and she wasn't very happy. She wasn't a person who went around soothing everybody. Now Lewis Lloyd, the vicar before Speakman, used to blow his top and tell everyone off but the

next day Mrs Lewis Lloyd used to go round and calm everybody down, but Mrs Speakman couldn't do that. I often feel that we let her down a bit. He was most inconsiderate. You see he'd fought in the First World War, then became a priest, a prison padre and went right through the second war. He was used to giving orders. Well it doesn't always work and she felt it.

I remember when she committed suicide. It was the day of the church fair in the church hall and the night before I saw her putting stalls up and she obviously wasn't very happy. She was putting the cloth on the stage table and usually you do that the following

Bolsover parish church choir was strong in numbers in the 1960s.

morning. She was ever so quiet and the next morning of course she did it, just before the fair opening. There was a cup of coffee on the table and she must have gone straight upstairs and committed suicide. He was the sort that doesn't react visibly, but obviously it must have shattered him. However, it wasn't obvious. Everybody was terribly shocked and blamed him. He certainly didn't help.

Bunty Margerrison

Mrs Speakman was a very quiet lady. She had some beautiful pieces of antique furniture which the Revd Speakman would sell without asking her. He used the money to take choir

and servers on holiday. I think she just decided she couldn't cope any longer.

Anne Joyce

Sunday School Anniversaries

We used to have Sunday School Treat in the fields where Hides Green is. We used to carry the sandwiches and the buns in a basket covered with a tablecloth and something to drink. We had races and more often than not you landed in a cow pat!

For Sunday School Anniversary you practised for weeks. You went round the town in the early morning, then you

'*Messiah* in costume' at the Congregational church. Joyce Leaning is second from the left, second row from the back.

had a morning service, then the afternoon one and evening one too; it wasn't half a hard day. Everyone had a new dress, a white one if you could afford it. There was a harmonium on a lorry or a dray and you stopped at various places, sang and collected. The chapels were absolutely packed. I remember at Town End once, Mrs Vann, a teacher at Welbeck Road and then at the 'Nats' until she retired, very musical she was, and she got all us children singing the *Hallelujah Chorus* and it was beautiful. You even had people sitting on the platform then. They were so thrilled with it when it was all over they demanded we sing it again!

My father was a conductor for many years and he was very keen. You couldn't have hymn sheets, you had to know every word. As he was headmaster you did as you were told.

Joyce Leaning

Chapel Anniversary

We used to go down to the little chapel at Carr Vale twice a day, me and my brothers and sister, and we had a lovely anniversary; it used to be a treat, that did. On Anniversary Sunday we had a dray drawn by horses, with a little harmonium on it and go all round Carr Vale, Model Village and up to what used to be the Manager's house from the colliery, and sing. Then, back home, get your dinner, put your new

125

frock on and then up on the platform.

A.W.

'Big at Chapel'

The family at Sherwood Lodge were very smart, upper ten really. Mr Sykes was a proper gentleman farmer. They ran the chapel, it really belonged to them.

Kath Palmer

Church Duties

I was junior Sacristan at the parish church during the war when I was quite a young girl. My duties were to go down to the church, always on my bike, every night on weekdays, winter and summer. These were the days of the blackout, and I had to let myself into the church, put all the robes and vestments in order, depending on which saint's day it was. I would light the sanctuary lamp and let myself out again. You couldn't do that today as an unaccompanied girl, especially in the pitch black with no street lamps.

Pam Ashley

Harvest Time

Anne and I went to see Revd Speakman when we wished to get married. He gave us one of his little talks, all the time dropping cigarette ash down his front. When he'd finished he just chucked the end over his shoulder hoping it would hit the stove. During the talk he asked me if I'd been sowing my wild oats rather than attending church!

David Joyce

Counting the Faithful

Father Talmay at Scarcliffe church would stand up on Sunday and say, 'Well, there are forty people here, where are all the rest?' And he wanted to know!

Norah Ley

Sunday School Treats

Sunday School Treat at Christmas was really great. We used to have tea laid out in chapel and were given an apple and oranges. In the summer food was packed into old fashioned clothes baskets and we went down to the Doe Lea for a picnic and the weather always seemed to be good. We used to paddle down Water Lane.

A.W.

Church Fêtes

I remember making a lampshade for the church fête and decorating it with acorns and being very proud, as a youngster. Mrs Lewis Lloyd bought it and put it in the vicar's study and I thought that was something great. It just shows you how simple things

A Town End chapel tea in the 1960s.

pleased us in those days. I can't imagine it happening today.

Pam Ashley

Messiah in Costume

We did Messiah in costume, dramatized at the Congregational church, and Mrs Hoten arranged it. She was wife of Sydney Hoten, the council surveyor and very musical. She'd seen this somewhere else and thought we could do it in Bolsover and so she got all the chapels interested and we all joined together for this dramatized version of Messiah in costume. It ran for a week and was really marvellous. Mary Hunts' father, the farmer, took his dog and sat at the front! I was an angel along with four others in floaty blue muslin. It was lovely.

Joyce Leaning

Church Fire in 1897...

Uncle John always had a horse and he used to tell us of the time when Bolsover church was burnt down in 1897 and he had to gallop off to Welbeck to fetch the fire brigade. It was a snowy, icy January morning and there was no fire appliance in Bolsover at all. Mother was living with two aunts on High Street at the time and she remembers the fire. Uncle was Chief Engineer on the tunnel at Carr Vale. He was from the Lake District.

Ada Bagshaw

...And 1960

On the day of the church fire in 1960 we were coming back from Worksop and there was snow on the ground. On approaching Bolsover we could see this great pall of smoke everywhere, it was the church. People were standing around crying. I think it started as an electrical fault in the organ loft.

Pam Ashley

Church Divisions

My grandfather was a strict Congregationalist, but his son, my father, had to attend the Church of England school as it was the only one in the town. However, on holy days when the children attended parish church service we were instructed by grandfather that when walking between school and church, on passing Cotton Street we had to leave the crocodile of children and then slip off home!

Even when I was at school when Vicar Lewis Lloyd came to teach religious instruction my father was so concerned that I should not receive C. of E. doctrine that he wrote to the headmaster requesting that I should be excluded from such lessons.

Margaret Utridge

Visiting the Monks

Revd Lewis Lloyd was keen on walking and would take young people from the church out to Edale and up Mam Tor and Jacob's Ladder. We'd travel on the Hulley's bus.

He also took us to Kelham near Newark which was an Anglican monastery belonging to the Society of the Resurrection in Yorkshire. I remember it was summer and the monks

wore shorts with an over tunic. The boys were taken around to see the monks' quarters but the girls weren't allowed there. I don't know what they expected us to see!

Pam Ashley

How We Remember It

Sunday school was so very boring. It consisted of untrained straight-laced maiden ladies telling Bible stories and getting you to draw pictures. Awful!

Anne Joyce

St Winifred's

I was a Church of England man, and went to St Winifred's, where the garage is now. My mother said, 'You're going!' and we had to go! We daren't argue and somebody tempted me to go to the parish church and I was going afternoon and evening. Paget was the vicar. I still go every three weeks. Vicar Speakman was a keen fellow.

Alf Bentley